COUNTERING TRUTH DECAY A RAND Initiative to Restore the Role of Facts and Analysis in Public Life

DEFINING AND MEASURING CIVIC INFRASTRUCTURE

JULIA H. KAUFMAN I MELISSA KAY DILIBERTI
DOUGLAS YEUNG I JENNIFER KAVANAGH

For more information on this publication, visit **www.rand.org/t/RRA112-24**.

About RAND

The RAND Corporation is a research organization that develops solutions to public policy challenges to help make communities throughout the world safer and more secure, healthier and more prosperous. RAND is nonprofit, nonpartisan, and committed to the public interest. To learn more about RAND, visit www.rand.org.

Research Integrity

Our mission to help improve policy and decisionmaking through research and analysis is enabled through our core values of quality and objectivity and our unwavering commitment to the highest level of integrity and ethical behavior. To help ensure our research and analysis are rigorous, objective, and nonpartisan, we subject our research publications to a robust and exacting quality-assurance process; avoid both the appearance and reality of financial and other conflicts of interest through staff training, project screening, and a policy of mandatory disclosure; and pursue transparency in our research engagements through our commitment to the open publication of our research findings and recommendations, disclosure of the source of funding of published research, and policies to ensure intellectual independence. For more information, visit www.rand.org/about/research-integrity.

RAND's publications do not necessarily reflect the opinions of its research clients and sponsors.

Published by the RAND Corporation, Santa Monica, Calif.
© 2022 RAND Corporation
RAND® is a registered trademark.

Library of Congress Cataloging-in-Publication Data is available for this publication.

ISBN: 978-1-9774-1034-4

Cover design: Pete Soriano
Cover image: CSA-Printstock/Getty Images

About This Report

Is U.S. democracy at risk or just shifting and evolving? Are the civic ties that bind citizens together as Americans fraying or reconstituting themselves in new ways? Recent events and trends—such as the January 6, 2021, attack on the U.S. Capitol; Black Lives Matter protests; and growing levels of misinformation and disinformation disseminated online—illustrate that the United States is in a complex and challenging moment in its history. Scholars and policy organizations have taken these and other factors as evidence that the United States needs a civic renewal.

These concerns about U.S. democracy are understandable. However, whether the United States requires a civic renewal is an open question. **It is not possible to know whether civic infrastructure needs repair, nor how to repair it, unless robust measures can be defined and applied to monitor it over time and across contexts.** Although some organizations have developed measures of civic health that could reflect the state of U.S. civic infrastructure, those measures are considerably broad, and they function more as comprehensive lists of factors that could support civic infrastructure than as a definition of civic infrastructure and its intended goals.

This report offers a framework for defining and measuring civic infrastructure and presents some measures that provide information to help monitor civic infrastructure across the United States, in individual states, in communities, and across diverse populations. The authors specifically define *civic infrastructure* as the places, policies, programs, and practices that undergird strong communities and foster civic engagement. The framework categorizes these places, policies, programs, and practices in terms of three inputs: (1) democratic governance, (2) civic education, and (3) civic spaces. The authors also consider how these inputs are related to a set of intertwined outputs: (1) civic literacy, (2) civic identity, and (3) civic engagement.

This work is part of the RAND Corporation's Truth Decay initiative (Kavanagh and Rich, 2018), which studies the diminishing role of facts and analysis in public life. Through this initiative, RAND has invited researchers and engaged stakeholders to find solutions that counter Truth Decay and the threat it poses to evidence-based policymaking. More information about Truth Decay is available at www.rand.org/truth-decay. More information about RAND can be found at www.rand.org. Questions about this report should be directed to jkaufman@rand.org.

Funding

Funding for this research was provided by gifts from RAND supporters and income from operations.

Acknowledgments

The authors would like to thank a long list of individuals who have contributed their ideas to various versions of this report. First, many thanks to Jhacova Williams, who provided regular input on our framework and measures. In addition, thanks to Anita Chandra, Katherine Carman, Celia Gomez, Debra Knopman, Michael Pollard, Osonde Osoba, and Lisa Saum-Manning for the initial review of and input regarding our civic infrastructure definition. Further thanks to Anita and Katherine, along with Marek Posard, for their additional reviews and comments on a draft of our report. Thanks also to our peer reviewers—Kei Kawashima-Ginsberg and Christopher Nelson—who provided constructive feedback that improved our report. We are also grateful to Arwen Bicknell and Monette Velasco, who provided expert editing and project management assistance for this publication.

Summary

In this report, we offer a framework for defining and measuring civic infrastructure. We then present some measures that are well aligned with our definition and provide information to help monitor civic infrastructure across the United States, in individual states, in communities, and across diverse populations. We specifically define *civic infrastructure* as the places, policies, programs, and practices that undergird strong communities and foster civic engagement. Our framework categorizes these places, policies, programs, and practices in terms of three inputs: (1) democratic governance, (2) civic education, and (3) civic spaces. In contrast with previous definitions of civic infrastructure, we also consider how these inputs are related to a set of intertwined outputs: (1) civic literacy, (2) civic identity, and (3) civic engagement. We define each of these inputs and outputs that are part of our framework in more detail in the first chapter of this report.

In the second chapter, we identify a set of measures for the inputs and outputs in our framework. These measures were selected using six criteria:

- evidence of content validity
- transparent methodology
- comparability over time
- comparability across geographical areas
- comparability across subgroups
- availability of raw data for researchers to access.

At a minimum, we sought measures that met our standards for content validity, provided a transparent methodology, and met at least one of the other criteria.

The following are research questions and key findings from our work:

- **What aspects of U.S. civic infrastructure that align with our framework are (and are not) measured?**
  - Aspects of civic infrastructure that are covered most comprehensively are those related to political participation.

- Measures provide some indication of international variation in democratic governance and transparency across countries, but state-by-state data and local data—critical disaggregations given the decentralized nature of the U.S. system—are often lacking.
- Input measures that provide some information about state-by-state variation focus more on state policies and laws than on evidence of actual access or opportunities provided as they relate to a given input (for example, civic learning opportunities available in schools).
- **What do the measures we identified say about the strength of U.S. civic infrastructure?**
  - Several measures suggest a downturn in democratic governance over the past several years, although some civic engagement measures have ticked slightly upward in the past year or so.
  - In the past several years, there has been a proliferation of state legislation to either restrict or expand Americans' civil and political rights.
  - Relatedly, state-by-state variations across many inputs and outputs in our framework suggest unequal access to the opportunities that drive civic literacy, identity, and engagement in the United States. Specifically, the state and community in which a person lives likely determines much about that person's civic infrastructure.
  - Diversity of the population is expanding, yet diversity is lacking in critical areas of civic infrastructure.

This exploratory research has several limitations. We have not, for example, conducted any quantitative analysis examining relationships among the components in our civic infrastructure framework. In addition, although we did identify some useful measures aligned with our framework, we may have inadvertently overlooked others. Furthermore, almost all the measures we have identified have some drawbacks (in that they do not meet all our criteria) and so should be regarded only as examples and not always as the best ways to measure given constructs. Finally, our framework and measures are derived from conceptions and theories of democracy in general and from Western democracies more specifically. These measures may therefore be of limited usefulness in nondemocratic settings.

Despite these limitations, this work has some implications for research, policy, and practice. First, more research is needed to test and confirm our definition, framework, and measures. Second, federal and state policies could increase collection and availability of measures—for example, expanding nationally representative data sets to provide state representative data when possible, increasing the accessibility and standardization of data, and encouraging U.S. participation in international data collection activities. Lastly, our research suggests considerable variation across states and communities in regard to rights and access to many aspects of our civic infrastructure framework, from democratic governance, civic education, and civic spaces to the outputs of civic literacy, identity, and engagement we identified. For that reason, our work implies the urgent need for more efforts to measure equitable access to and participation in aspects of civic infrastructure, both to monitor the health of our democracy and to determine ways of improving it.

Contents

Figure and Tables

Figure

Tables

CHAPTER 1

The Case for Defining and Measuring Civic Infrastructure

Is American democracy at risk or just shifting and evolving? Are the civic ties that bind citizens together as Americans fraying or reconstituting themselves in new ways? Recent events and trends—such as the January 6, 2021, attack on the U.S. Capitol; Black Lives Matter protests; and growing levels of misinformation and disinformation disseminated online—illustrate that the United States is in a complex and challenging moment in its history. Scholars and policy organizations have taken these and other factors as evidence that the United States needs a civic renewal. According to the Commission on the Practice of Democratic Citizenship, "the profoundly challenging conditions of the twenty-first century pose an urgent threat to the future of our democratic way of life" (Commission on the Practice of Democratic Citizenship, 2020, p. 3). The commission called for urgent actions to empower voters and improve equality of voice and representation, among numerous other recommendations. These recommendations echo calls from the Aspen Institute for the formation of a "21st Century Civic Infrastructure," noting that infrastructure from the past century may be "damaging or undermining or compromising our potential for positive social impact" (Blair and Kopell, 2015, p. 5).

Michael D. Rich and Jennifer Kavanagh (2020) have similarly called for strengthening civic infrastructure in the name of countering Truth Decay—a set of converging trends that the RAND Corporation and others have tracked in recent years, such as increased disagreement about facts and data, a blurring of the line between opinion and fact, an increase in the relative volume and resulting influence of opinion and personal experience over fact, and a lowered trust in formerly respected sources of information

(Kavanagh et al., 2020; Kavanagh and Rich, 2018; Pollard and Kavanagh, 2019). Kavanagh and Rich (2018) named not only drivers of these trends—cognitive biases, polarization, and aspects of both information and education systems—but also concerning potential consequences—erosion of civil discourse, political and social disengagement, and political partisanship and gridlock.

These concerns about U.S. democracy are understandable. However, whether America requires a civic renewal is an open question. Alarm bells about civic infrastructure and civic ties have been raised numerous times over the past 50 or more years. In 1979, B. J. Allen wrote, "There is a civic crisis in America," citing declining rates of voting and public trust in government and social institutions since the mid-1960s (Allen, 1979). In the early 1990s, John Parr—then president of the National Civic League—used the term "civic infrastructure" to call out the important role of civic associations and traditions in the face of decreasing funding for societal needs and increasing population diversity along with potential for growing polarization (Parr, 1993). In response to these concerning trends, the National Civic League developed the National Civic Index to help communities measure and improve their "civic capital" in order to advance better local decision-making and collaboration (Gates, 1987).

In 2000, Robert Putnam amplified concerns about the need for community and civic associations, arguing that Americans were becoming increasingly isolated and that this isolation was driving a decline of physical and civic health (Putnam, 2000). Putnam's research has since been critiqued for its empirical shortcomings (Boggs, 2001; Durlauf, 2002), including his attention to particular metrics over others (for example, focusing on participation in civic associations but ignoring various other types of social participation proliferating at that time). On the other hand, Putnam's work, in part, helped to drive efforts by the National Conference on Citizenship (NCOC) to formulate the Civic Health Index (NCOC, 2006), a set of indicators to measure civic health across multiple categories, such as connections to civic groups, family, friends, and institutions; trust in people; extent of giving and volunteering; understanding of civics and politics; participation in politics; and expression of political views. In its work, NCOC has noted continuing declines in connections among people and organizations—as

Putnam also found—as well as declines in trust and being informed regarding political affairs (NCOC, 2006; Atwell, Stillerman, and Bridgeland, 2021).

Although Putnam and such organizations as the National Civic League and NCOC have expressed grave concerns about growing polarization and lack of social cohesion, others have suggested that political and social conflict and divisiveness is a "feature of democracy, not a bug" (Skinnell, 2020). Moss argued that "democracy in America has always been a contact sport" and that it survives and flourishes "on the basis not principally of harmony but of conflict . . . mediated, generally, by shared ideals" (Moss, 2017, p. 3). Moss also said that the critical thing to figure out in periods of conflict is whether that conflict is "constructive or destructive" (Moss, 2017, p. 3). Similarly, Wood, Baen, and Cloke (2019) created a set of tools that support social change efforts to understand conflict engagement. In this view, conflict can bring people together and foster community building and vibrant civic life, which some might argue has been an outcome of the Black Lives Matter, Me Too, and other movements (Baskin-Sommers et al., 2021; Edrington and Lee, 2018; Manago et al., 2021).

It is not possible to know whether civic infrastructure needs repair, nor how to repair it, unless robust measures can be defined and applied to monitor it over time and across contexts. Although the National Civic League and NCOC have created measures of civic health that could reflect the state of U.S. civic infrastructure, those measures are considerably broad and function more as comprehensive lists of factors that could support civic infrastructure than a definition of civic infrastructure and its intended goals. Furthermore, although these organizations have applied these indexes to examine various areas of civic infrastructure nationally (in the case of NCOC) and in local communities (in the case of the National Civic League), their reports do not attempt to examine relationships among indicators (for example, which factors may be driving or may be proxies for other, more-critical aspects of civic infrastructure). Nor do they provide information about the strength of measures in each area of civic health that they have identified.

In this report, we take a step beyond these indexes to offer (1) a comprehensive definition and framework for civic infrastructure and (2) a roundup of the most-rigorous measures we could find that are aligned with our framework and could help monitor civic infrastructure across the United

States, in individual states, and in communities. The measures we identified offer data on areas that align with our definition of civic infrastructure and on areas where critical measures are lacking. In addition, the measures themselves provide some suggestions about where civic infrastructure may be weaker or stronger. Overall, these data have implications for additional research, policies, and practices that can help monitor the health of civic infrastructure and democracy and identify ways to improve it.

This report is aimed at several audiences: (1) researchers who could further delve into better understanding U.S. civic infrastructure and drivers of civic engagement; (2) federal and state policymakers who want to monitor and improve civic infrastructure across the United States and in their particular locale; (3) local leaders who want to hone in on key aspects of civic infrastructure that they could build on and improve in their own communities; and (4) nonprofits and other organizations looking for concrete ways to partner with communities to strengthen civic health. In the conclusion of this report, we provide more-detailed information for how all these audiences might come together to strengthen civic infrastructure and the foundations of U.S. democracy.

This work is just a starting point. By defining civic infrastructure and identifying possible measures to monitor it, we hope to catalyze funding and efforts to better track the health of civic infrastructure over time and to identify areas most in need of investment. In the remainder of this chapter, we discuss some definitions of civic infrastructure and then introduce the civic infrastructure framework we use in this report. In Chapter 2, we share information on measures of civic infrastructure and identify areas that have robust civic infrastructure measures and areas that do not. In addition, we briefly consider what these measures say about the state of civic infrastructure. Lastly, in Chapter 3, we share some recommendations for research, policy, and practice that are based on our investigation.

Definitions of Civic Infrastructure

Several scholars have explicitly studied civic infrastructure in the United States and other countries and attempted to define it. Patrick and Brady (2015), for example, termed *civic infrastructure* as "the foundation on which ordinary people participate in ordinary civic life . . . . It is the places, policies, programs, and practices that enable us to connect with each other, define and address shared concerns, build community, and solve public problems." Twenty years prior, Parr defined the term as "the individual structures and processes through which the social contract is written and rewritten in communities . . . the formal and informal processes and networks through which communities make decisions and solve problems" (Parr, 1993, p. 93). Parr's work was the basis for the National Civic League's *Civic Index* (2019), which was intended to help communities empower themselves by evaluating and improving their civic infrastructure. The Civic Index provided tools for communities to measure numerous aspects of civic health, such as citizenship participation, community leadership, government performance, volunteerism and philanthropy, civic education, and intercommunity cooperation, among other factors.

Other researchers may not have used the term *civic infrastructure* for what they investigated but nonetheless were examining similar aspects of civic life. For example, Putnam, Leonardi, and Nanetti (1994) studied the factors that influenced good democratic governance in various regions of Italy, and they concluded that strong democratic governance depends on trust and cooperation among its citizenry. Sirianni and Friedland (2001) wrote of "civic innovation" as "mobilizing social capital in ways that promote broad democratic norms, enhance responsible and inclusive citizenship, and build the civic capacities of communities and institutions to solve problems through the public work of citizens themselves" (pp. 13–14). Some research has more narrowly defined *civic capital* or *civic infrastructure* as ties among various types of organizations and individuals that facilitate community or city development (Bogart, 2003; Wolfe, 2012) or even just as the broadband or online connections that support civic engagement (McShane, Wilson, and Meredyth, 2014; Thorson, Xu, and Edgerly, 2018). For example, the Reimagining the Civic Commons initiative developed a set of tools designed to measure the presence and use of public spaces as a way to support civic engagement, socioeconomic mixing, environmental sustainability, and value creation; some of its tools are measures of public life and social networks (Reimagining the Civic Commons, 2018). In another example, Welcoming America created a toolkit to help communities better welcome newcomers to the United States and support social cohesion among all community members (Downs-Karkos and Peric, 2019).

NCOC releases regular reports on civic health, which it defines as encompassing "all the ways citizens are connected with one another, with their institutions, and with other organizations and groups" (NCOC, undated). In its most-recent civic health report, NCOC—along with the University of Virginia's Miller Center and Democracy Initiative and the Partnership for American Democracy—notes trends in an array of areas: voting, public trust in government, volunteerism, religious attendance, and union membership (Atwell, Stillerman, and Bridgeland, 2021). However, the report does not make clear which of these may be better or worse indicators of civic health. The National Civic League (2019) also relies on a broad definition of civic infrastructure—which it refers to as *civic capital*—that factors in such items as shared vision and values, authentic communication, and embracing diversity and equity. Furthermore, the National Civic League provides excellent tools and ideas for how communities can use the index to measure civic capital in their locale, although it does not attempt to gauge the strength of civic health nationally, as the NCOC has done.

Framework for Defining Civic Infrastructure

Although we support these previous efforts to define civic infrastructure, we argue that prior research does not provide the tools to measure varied aspects of civic infrastructure at scale, over time, and in a robust way. By developing such measures of civic infrastructure, it might be possible to move closer to being able to track the health of civic infrastructure over time and to compare it across contexts (for example, states, regions) and subgroups of people (for example, by race, gender, age, and socioeconomic status). In addition, previous definitions have not attempted to separate the various aspects of civic infrastructure, which could allow unpacking and exploration of the relationships among those aspects and how they coalesce (or not) to support a robust civic infrastructure. See the box for the methods we used to define civic infrastructure.

For this report, we define *civic infrastructure* similarly to Patrick and Brady (2015)—as the "places, policies, programs, and practices" that under-

Our Methods

We drew on a review of literature and consultation with experts to develop our definition of *civic infrastructure*. In our review, we started by searching for studies on the concept of civic infrastructure and branched out to search for studies on complementary concepts, such as civic capital and community infrastructure. Through that initial research, we developed a preliminary definition of civic infrastructure that we shared with an array of RAND experts in such disciplines as political science, social science, and information science. Using their feedback, we further refined our definition to focus on the key aspects of civic infrastructure illustrated in Figure 1.1. We then conducted further literature review to identify studies in each area of our framework along with studies investigating relationships among the inputs and outputs in our definition.

gird strong communities and foster civic engagement. We expand on that definition to provide a comprehensive framework for what those places, policies, programs, and practices include. Our framework for civic infrastructure consists of three key inputs: (1) democratic governance, (2) civic education, and (3) civic spaces. In contrast to previous definitions, we also consider how those inputs may be connected with a set of intertwined outputs: (1) civic literacy, (2) civic identity, and (3) civic engagement. This framework—as with the definitions we have already cited—draws on ideas of citizenship that are explicitly democratic, in terms of existing in a form of government where at least some political power resides with citizens.

Figure 1.1 illustrates our framework, which was developed and refined through consultation with experts in political science, social science, and several other disciplines; it is not exhaustive or inclusive of all the inputs that keep our democracy healthy but does show many of the key factors that have been described in other research.

The outputs (civic literacy, civic identity, and civic engagement) in our framework are intended to represent the knowledge, perceptions, and actions that reflect and support participation in our democracy. The inputs (democratic governance, civic education, and civic spaces) represent concepts and opportunities closely associated with these outputs in our literature review. Democratic governance, in particular, is the necessary con-

FIGURE 1.1

Our Civic Infrastructure Framework

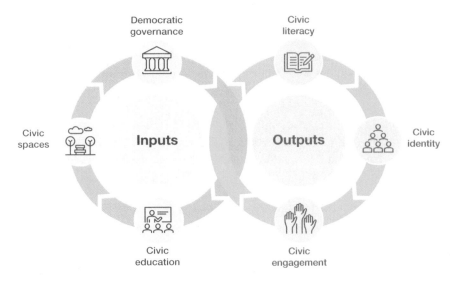

text for high-quality civic education, along with the formation of civic spaces. Without a democracy that has democratic policies and guardrails (for example, free and fair elections, transparency of governance, and laws allowing for critical dissent), civic education and civic spaces will not flourish. In our definition, civic education is critical to supporting civic literacy as well as individuals' and groups' civic identity and engagement. At the same time, civic spaces are a key context for individuals to practice civic skills and learn how to better engage civically. In contrast with other definitions, ours does not include concepts capturing generic social or human connections (for example, social capital) as part of our civic infrastructure. We made this choice because social connections are not clear predictors of greater civic knowledge, identity, or engagement in all cases (for example, see Liu, Austin, and Orey, 2009; Rydgren, 2009). In fact, tight social connections may actually be negative predictors of democratic engagement in some contexts (Shah, Kwak, and Holbert, 2001; van Deth and Zmerli, 2010). For these reasons, and in contrast with measures of collaboration, social capital, and engagement in other indices (for example, the National Civic League and NCOC), we consider social connections and related concepts as important context for, but not explicit elements of, civic infrastructure.

Definitions of Six Key Components in Our Civic Infrastructure Framework

Inputs

- **Democratic governance:** Essential elements of democracy, including respect for human rights and fundamental freedoms; rule of law; free and fair elections; pluralistic system of political parties; separation of powers and independence of judiciary; transparency and accountability in public administration; and a free, independent, and pluralistic media.
- **Civic education:** Policies, practices, and opportunities that support individuals to develop and grow their civic knowledge, skills, and dispositions.
- **Civic spaces:** Physical or virtual places where citizens can come together to engage in civic discourse and activities.

Outputs

- **Civic literacy:** Knowledge and skills necessary to participate effectively in civic life.
- **Civic identity:** Beliefs and dispositions that form personal and group identities related to participation in civic life, such as political leaning, civic duty, self-efficacy, feelings of social or civic responsibility, and sense of belonging within a country, state, or community.
- **Civic engagement:** Individuals' participation in civic life—community service, electoral activities, and/or activities intended to drive social change.

In the remainder of this chapter, we define these constructs in more detail; a brief definition for each is offered in the box.

We posit that this framework is applicable at multiple geographic levels. It could be used to consider civic infrastructure across the entire United States, within individual states, or within local communities. At the same time, the relationships between these interlocking inputs and outputs are likely different depending on the demographics and needs within a given community. Specifically, a variety of contextual conditions likely play a role in whether—for example—individuals have interest in or access to civic spaces and education. Similarly, different states across the country have widely varying histories, laws, and policies that afford a variety of opportunities in terms of civic engagement. We thus hypothesize that these inputs and outputs are dynamic and changing over time and space, both related to one another and to the populations in particular communities.

Democratic Governance

Defining Democratic Governance. Democratic governance is a cornerstone and foundation for civic outcomes. Such governance is intertwined with the other two inputs in our infrastructure definition: civic education and civic spaces. There is not one global definition of democracy, but liberty (that is, the ability of individuals to have control over their lives) and equality (that is, all people having the same status, rights, and opportunities) are typically noted as key principles of democratic governance. Freedom House (undated-e)—an independent, nonpartisan organization[1]—rates "Global Freedom" in 195 countries, including the United States; the ratings focus on political rights and civil liberties. The United Nations General Assembly provides a more comprehensive list of essential elements of a democracy that we use to define democratic governance for this report:

- Respect for human rights and fundamental freedoms
- Freedom of association
- Freedom of expression and opinion
- Access to power and its exercise in accordance with the rule of law

---

[1] Freedom House's methodology (Repucci and Slipowitz, 2022) is largely derived from standards set by the Universal Declaration of Human Rights (United Nations, 1948), draws on a wide variety of sources, and represents consensus across hundreds of analysts and advisers. The aspects of governance that they rate that are closely connected with civic outcomes (literacy, identity, and engagement) are (1) political rights focused on free and fair electoral processes and political participation and (2) civil liberties focused on freedom of expression and belief, associational rights, rule of law, and personal autonomy.

- The holding of periodic free and fair elections by universal suffrage and by secret ballot as the expression of the will of the people
- A pluralistic system of political parties and organizations
- The separation of powers
- The independence of the judiciary
- Transparency and accountability in public administration
- Free, independent and pluralistic media. (United Nations, undated)

This definition of democratic governance is intentionally broad enough to be applied both within and outside the United States, although some of the measures of democratic governance that we identify in the next chapter are more U.S.-centric in that they focus on state-by-state differences in laws and policies. The Tenth Amendment of the U.S. Constitution specifically gives states—not the federal government—decisionmaking authority over the organization of local government, and states have designated multiple systems of local government, such as county, township, and municipal governments. Thus, the power of central governance in the United States is perceived as somewhat weaker than the central power in most other democratic nations (such as many in Europe), and U.S. residents have more-proximal experiences with government than their counterparts in many other democratic nations (for example, town meetings and the like) (John and Cole, 1988; Townsend, 2009; Zimmerman, 1999). For these reasons, our framework for civic infrastructure may be more easily applied at state and local levels in the United States than in other countries.

Relationships Between Democratic Governance and Civic Literacy, Identity, and Engagement. Several factors have tied aspects of democratic governance to the key outputs in our model of civic infrastructure: civic literacy, identity, and engagement. As might be expected, electoral laws that involve compulsory voting, electoral competition, and proportional representation in governance have strong relationships to voter participation in cross-national studies (Dalton, Farrell, and McAllister, 2011; Franklin, 1999; Jackman, 1987).

A survey of local government officials across the United States in 2010 found close ties between transparency—defined as *information dissemination*—and political participation (Feeney, Welch, and Haller,

2011). Some research notes that transparency can reduce corruption in government (Montinola and Jackman, 2002; Rose-Ackerman, 2012). However, interestingly, transparency can also lead to the deterioration of trust, particularly in societies where corruption is high (Bauhr, Grimes, and Harring, 2010).

Although not an objective measure of the extent of democratic governance, perceptions of fairness of governance have also been tied to higher levels of civic identity and engagement (Doherty and Wolak, 2012; Miles, 2015), which are intertwined with income inequality and racial violence (van Holm, 2019; Williams, Logan, and Hardy, 2021). Research has also linked diversity of representation (that is, that representation in governance is equitable and matches the population) with higher perceptions of fairness (Lawless, 2004; Riccucci and Van Ryzin, 2017; Tate, 2004; Theobald and Haider-Markel, 2008).

Civic Education

Defining Civic Education. Civic education encompasses academic standards and requirements for civic education, along with the opportunities that individuals have to develop and grow civically—both formal learning opportunities in kindergarten through 12th grade (K–12) and higher education settings and informal learning opportunities outside the school system (Hansen et al., 2018; Vinnakota, 2019). Civic education scholars have identified a set of school and teacher practices in K–12 settings that support students' civic education and development, starting with traditional classroom instruction in civics, government, and other social studies subjects but also encompassing—more broadly—discussion of current and controversial issues, service learning, extracurricular activities, student participation in school governance, democratic simulations in class (for example, debates), news media literacy, action civics, social and emotional learning, and promotion of a positive school climate (Hansen et al., 2018; Huguet et al., 2019; Gould, 2011; Levine and Kawashima-Ginsberg, 2017). For example, the Democracy Schools Initiative in Illinois stresses not only the importance of emphasizing core civics concepts and active, student-centered practices within the classroom but also service learning and extracurricular activities that foster civic learning and engagement (Illinois Civic Hub, undated).

Civic learning opportunities likely vary widely across K–12 schools, given that states have considerably varied civic education standards, requirements for civic courses, media literacy, and assessments that focus on civic learning (Hansen et al., 2018). Typically, state civic education requirements for K–12 schools are integrated within broader social studies requirements encompassing other topics, particularly U.S. history. In their recent review of civics and U.S. history standards, Stern et al. (2021) noted a handful of states that do not have U.S. history standards at all and several where such standards are vague and briefly mentioned.

In addition to varying considerably across states, K–12 school offerings in civic education—and social studies more broadly—have likely been curtailed by schools' growing focus on student achievement in mathematics and English language arts. Since the advent of No Child Left Behind, which was signed into law in 2001, states have implemented high-stakes testing in reading and math in grades 3 through 8. Many U.S. educators and other stakeholders are in agreement that pressure for schools to improve reading and math has come at the expense of civic education (Council of Chief State School Officers, 2018; Hamilton, Kaufman, and Hu, 2020; Vinnakota, 2019). Furthermore, research has documented a declining focus on social studies and civic-related topics, particularly in elementary school (Heafner and Fitchett, 2012; Pace, 2011). Furthermore, states and districts began passing regulations in mid-2021 limiting discussions related to race, gender, and systematic inequality in U.S. schools—topics likely to be covered in social studies and civics classrooms (Schwartz, 2022). Although it is yet to be determined how much these regulations will affect social studies and civic instruction, nearly one-half of district superintendents reported in spring 2022 that political polarization related to Critical Race Theory was interfering with schooling and presumably with students' civic learning (Diliberti and Schwartz, 2022).

Relationships Between Civic Education and Civic Literacy, Identity, and Engagement. A growing body of evidence demonstrates that systematic civic learning opportunities in K–12 schools—such as taking courses in civics, service learning, and other civic activities at school—can lead to an increased likelihood of voting, participation in community service, and planned commitments to civic participation (Hart et al., 2007; Kahne and Sporte, 2008; Levine and Kawashima-Ginsberg, 2017). Research indicates that discussion of current events and controversial issues, democratic simulations, and action civics approaches can cultivate openness to difference and promote students' civic outcomes at school (Hansen et al., 2018; Huguet et al., 2019; Kahne and Sporte, 2008; Levine and Kawashima-Ginsberg, 2017). School interventions focused on developing students' "civic online reasoning" have also been tied to increased ability for students to navigate online effectively and identify reliable sources of information (McGrew et al., 2018), a key citizenship skill in a healthy democracy.

Access to high-quality civic learning opportunities in K–12 schools may depend on where students live, who their teachers are, and what school they attend. In their national survey of U.S. K–12 social studies teachers, Hamilton, Kaufman, and Hu (2020) found that teachers' reported emphasis on particular civics topics was greater for teachers who reported receiving any pre-service or in-service training to support students' civic development or were aware of state academic standards related to civic development. The researchers also found that teachers of color were more likely to emphasize particular topics that may intersect with race and culture, such as controversial issues, global community and international relations, respect for the environment, and immigration and emigration. Lastly, and importantly, schools serving higher percentages of students of color and low-income students were significantly less likely to report schoolwide emphasis on student participation in school governance and less likely to discuss controversial issues in the classroom.

Beyond K–12 education, formal civic learning opportunities extend to postsecondary education, although emphasis on supporting students' civic knowledge and competencies can vary widely by higher education institution and students' chosen area of study (Torney-Purta et al., 2015). Furthermore, civic development opportunities can be offered outside formal learning settings, although such opportunities are not widespread. For example, studies have demonstrated how opportunities for political deliberation—for example, systems for individuals to discuss public issues and politics—can improve political knowledge and participation (Fishkin and Luskin, 1999; Luskin, Fishkin, and Jowell, 2002), as well as their reasoning abilities (Price, Cappella, and Nir, 2002). Democracy initiatives and volunteer opportunities can provide citizenship and civic education to their participants (Kukovetz and Sprung, 2021; Schugurensky and Myers, 2008), as can interactions with parents and peers (Lauglo, 2011; Mellor, 2010). Relatedly, some research has explored how to design technology (for example, on social media) to support civic engagement, particularly among youth—such as functions that support participation and sharing, ability to engage in deliberation, and collaboration (Brandtzæg, Følstad, and Mainsah, 2012; Gordon and Mihailidis, 2016), as well as opportunities for friction among diverse voices and the ability to critique one another thoughtfully (Korn and Voida, 2015).

Civic Spaces

Defining Civic Spaces. Civic spaces include places—typically open to the public—where any individuals within a community can come together to engage in civic discourse and participate in civic activities, along with the laws or policies that support access and use of those spaces for civic purposes. Participatory democracy hinges on some form of public political participation by individuals in that democracy, and both physical and online sites for political participation can be conceived as civic spaces. Our concept of civic spaces, although more focused on explicit civic discourse, is akin to the conceptualization in Evans and Boyte (1992), which focuses on "free space" where members of a society or community come together in voluntary associations or other public places to share ideas and learn skills that will help them hone their democratic skills.

Physical civic spaces include those available for legislative and political activities (for example, town halls, legislative chambers, lawmaker offices, or sites of protest). Many organizations in the United States consider ways in which physical civic spaces can be developed to serve as extensions of a given community. The Project for Public Spaces (undated), for example, is a nonprofit organization that plans and designs public spaces with the goal of strengthening communities. As another example, Reimagining the Civic Commons (2018) has developed measurement systems for developing and supporting physical spaces in communities that foster civic engagement, socioeconomic mixing, environmental sustainability, and value creation. Some of the signals that this group has identified as part of that measurement system for aspects of public spaces that foster civic engagement are extent of public life or use in those spaces, stewardship or advocacy related to use of sites, and perceptions of trust within the neighborhoods where sites are located.

Virtual, or online, civic spaces are any platforms or websites where people can engage in democratic deliberation in their community and beyond. Some national and local governments have begun using online, open-source platforms as civic spaces for their constituents to engage in democratic deliberation and discourse; more such platforms proliferated during the coronavirus disease 2019 (COVID-19) pandemic (Gros and Eisen, 2021). For example, Decidim.org is an open-source platform that is now being used by many organizations and cities in Europe to support civic engagement. Other platforms, such as DemocraciaOS.org and Granicus.com, similarly support such deliberation. Hallmarks of such tools—based on recommendations from such organizations as the Open Government Partnership (2021)—are financial and reporting transparency, accountability through advisory and independent oversight processes, and inclusive protections and supports to ensure wide participation.

The internet can also serve as a platform that encourages or discourages civic spaces by supporting or curtailing online access or freedoms. Freedom House conducts an annual survey on internet freedom around the world and ranks online freedom by country. Among the measures that the group used to assess online freedoms in its most-recent report (Freedom House, undated-d) are (1) obstacles to internet access; (2) any limits on internet content via legal regulations, technical filtering and blocking, or other forms of censorship (including those that affect the "vibrancy and diversity" of online information space); and (3) violations of user rights to free expression and privacy.

Civic spaces can take multiple forms. The following are some examples of various types of civic spaces:

- *Open spaces* are civic spaces that are completely public, meaning access is entirely unrestricted, and are free to enter and use in a variety of ways.
- *Affinity spaces* are civic spaces in which access may be either open or by invitation. In a healthy civic infrastructure, the ability to form invite-only groups is available to all groups, meaning that any affinity group or community of interest can have access to specialized and more-intimate spaces of some kind when they are interested.

- *Civic institution spaces* provide access to opportunity to participate in civic processes and to engage with civic institutions. These may require deliberate effort to construct and sustain (for example, civic officials making themselves available to the public). They can offer a sense of agency within civic participation and civic engagement.

Relationships Between Civic Spaces and Civic Literacy, Identity, and Engagement. Although a great deal of scholarship considers how we might define civic spaces, fewer research studies examine relationships among civic spaces and civic outputs as we have defined them. Some studies have identified positive relationships among common spaces, community attachment, and social ties (for example, Arnberger and Eder, 2012; Kuo et al., 1998). Other research has begun to more closely examine how newspaper deserts affect local news journalism and community connections (Mathews, 2022; Miller, 2018).

Many more-recent studies have examined how virtual civic spaces support community engagement. Use of online social media has been linked to greater political participation and civic engagement (Bakker and de Vreese, 2011; Notley et al., 2021; Valenzuela, Kim, and Gil de Zúñiga, 2011; Ye, Xu, and Zhang, 2017), potentially because even social media use for nonpolitical purposes can involve some political disagreement (Wojcieszak and Mutz, 2009). Some studies also suggest that internet and social media use can support social bonds and community civic engagement offline (Ellison, Steinfield, and Lampe, 2007; Ognyanova et al., 2013).

Several studies have noted strong associations between internet access and exposure to campaign and election information, as well as feelings of political efficacy, knowledge, and participation (Chae, Lee and Kim, 2019; Kenski and Stroud, 2006; Tolbert and McNeal, 2003), and these associations are likely moderated by the relative disadvantage of those who do not have internet access, as well as government limitations to internet access. Ideological homophily among users of particular platforms can drive the opinions and content that individuals are exposed to on social media, even if those platforms were not specifically designed to support people of those specific demographics (Daniels, 2009; Tynes et al., 2011). Such homophily can create biases and discourage both access to and use of civic spaces.

Civic Outcomes

The key outputs for civic infrastructure in our definition are civic literacy, civic identity, and civic engagement, which are often intertwined and inter-related in the research literature. We define each in more detail.

Civic literacy encompasses civic knowledge and civic skills (Hansen et al., 2018; Vinnakota, 2019). By *civic knowledge*, we mean knowledge and understanding of government structure and processes, as well as relevant social studies knowledge and concepts, including U.S. and global history. By *civic skills*, we mean abilities that enable students to engage in democratic processes in an active and informed way, which could involve critical think-ing, communication, and collaboration, among other skills. Several studies have noted that civic literacy is closely intertwined with civic engagement, and higher levels of civic literacy have been associated with more involve-ment in electoral and political activities (Hylton, 2018), particularly when civic literacy is defined in terms of media literacy skills and knowledge (Ashley, Maksl, and Craft, 2017; Martens and Hobbs, 2015).

Civic identity is the set of beliefs, perceptions, and dispositions that form personal and group identities related to participating in civic life (Hart, Richardson, and Wilkenfeld, 2011; Petrovska, 2019). Studies that have attempted to capture information about civic identity have typically focused on three aspects: (1) attitudes toward political participation, includ-ing political self-efficacy, trust in governance, and political leaning (Gastil and Xenos, 2010; Moy and Scheufele, 2000); (2) feelings of civic or social duty and responsibility (Knefelkamp, 2008; Mabry, 1998; Mitchell, 2015); and (3) sense of belonging within and pride regarding one's country, state, or community (Lewicka, 2011).

Although studies have found close ties between civic attitudes and civic engagement, those relationships are complex and dependent on constructs being measured (Gastil and Xenos, 2010). For example, Gastil and Xenos (2010) found that civic pride (that is, a personal sense of pride in one's civic responsibility) was closely related to the likelihood of an individual talking to others about politics or their community, whereas civic faith (that is, faith in the responsibility of citizens) had a slight negative impact with reported voting rates.

Civic engagement has been defined in a wide variety of ways in the research literature (Adler and Goggin, 2005). Putnam (2000), for example, describes civic engagement in terms of any activities that build social capital, which he regards as any aspects of social organizations (for example, networks, norms, trust) that may be mutually beneficial to those involved. In contrast, some studies have focused on more-active examples of civic engagement, such as community service (Diller, 2001), collective action to improve society (Ebert and Okamoto, 2013; Levine, 2006), or specifically political activities, such as voting or other activities aimed at influencing political or governmental decisions (Brady, 1999; van Deth, 2001).

Drawing on Keeter et al. (2002) and similar conceptions of civic engagement (Ekman and Amnå, 2012), we define *civic engagement* in terms of (1) community service activities, such as volunteer efforts to feed the homeless; (2) electoral activities, such as voting; and (3) activities intended to drive political and social change, such as protesting, contacting public officials, supporting social movements. In their work to measure civic and political health, Keeter et al. (2002) surveyed a nationally representative sample of Americans ages 15 and over to gauge civic engagement according to 19 different indicators of engagement under three major umbrellas: civic indicators (for example, nonpolitical community participation), electoral indicators (for example, voting, volunteering for or contributing to political campaigns), and political voice indicators (for example, contacting public officials, protesting or petitioning, or boycotting). By this definition, the authors found that a little more than one-half of Americans were civically engaged in one form or another, with voting as the most common form of engagement.

In the next chapter, we use our civic infrastructure framework to identify robust measures to track the health of our civic infrastructure. We then consider both what we know already from those measures about the strength of our civic infrastructure and what measures are missing that keep us from providing a comprehensive assessment of that infrastructure.

CHAPTER 2

Measuring Civic Infrastructure

In this chapter, we present a series of measures associated with our civic infrastructure framework. These measures should not be interpreted as our ideal list of measures or as an exhaustive list of indicators to track the health of our civic infrastructure. Instead, we present measures that meet some of our minimum criteria for inclusion to give readers a lay of the land regarding potential measures of our civic infrastructure. For each input and output, we provide a table of these measures and briefly address the following questions:

- What is and is not captured in the United States through measures we have identified?
- What signals about civic infrastructure do these measures provide?

Our descriptions of what signals about civic infrastructure these measures provide are not meant to build a comprehensive or complete picture about the status of our civic infrastructure. This is outside the scope of this report. However, we use these sections to provide some general idea of big-picture patterns and as illustrative examples of the potential utility of these measures.

Selection Criteria for Measures

To identify measures, we conducted online (for example, Google, Google Scholar) searches of indicators related to our civic infrastructure definition.

To help determine which measures to include, we defined a set of key criteria that measures ideally would meet. Our six key criteria were:

- **Evidence of Content Validity:** Measures for each civic infrastructure input and output were closely related to our definitions for those inputs and outputs.
- **Transparent Methodology:** Measures were accompanied by transparent information on methods for establishing those measures and/or information about positive relationships between that measure and other variables related to civic infrastructure (for example, a relationship between a civic education measure and civic engagement).
- **Comparability over Time:** Ideally, measures would be updated on a regular basis such that they are able to capture meaningful changes in the measure over time.
- **Comparability Across Geographical Areas:** Country-by-country, state-by-state, county-by-county, or city-by-city comparisons would shed light on variation, including places with strong civic infrastructure that might merit more study and areas of weaker infrastructure that might be improved on.
- **Comparability Across Subgroups:** Ideal measures were disaggregated by subgroups (especially by race/ethnicity, gender, age, and socioeconomic status) to allow for monitoring of equitable access to civic infrastructure.
- **Raw Data Available for Researchers to Access:** Datasets used to produce these measures were easily and freely accessible for individuals and organizations to use and available in a format (for example, raw data files, data tools, databases) that allow people to easily conduct their own analyses. (For more information about how to access data on each measure, see Table A.1.)

At minimum, we sought measures that met our standards for content validity and at least some other validity or reliability evidence (for example, transparency about how measures were developed), along with at least one other criterion: comparability over time, comparability for more than one geographic level (that is, by country, state, or county/city), or comparability by subgroup. We viewed accessibility as a bonus attribute of the measures but did not exclude measures that might be harder for some individuals than others to access or to analyze.

We do not take into account the many ways in which measures could be merged with other measures to investigate data in more-nuanced ways. For example, some of the measures we identify are not separately reported by subgroups. However, many of those measures could be merged with demographic data from other sources, such as the U.S. Census Bureau's American Community Survey, to provide some information across subgroups. In this chapter, however, we focus on evaluating measures themselves, assuming that many users many will not have the time, resources, or skill set necessary to merge measures in this way.

Inputs

In the following tables, we list measures that met our criteria for the three inputs: democratic governance, civic education, and civic spaces. These measures generally fell into three main categories that we note in the tables: measures tracking particular types of laws and policies, measures attempting to capture equitable access related to a given input, or measures reflecting representation and actions among those who are expected to lead or undertake efforts related to a given input.

Democratic Governance

Democratic governance is deeply intertwined with such outputs as civic engagement, as well as the ideal goal of a strong civic infrastructure: a more participatory, representative, healthy democracy. The measures that we have listed (Table 2.1) are ones that we identified that both align with our content criteria and have validity evidence in more than one category that is included in our criteria. As we noted in the previous chapter, we define the essential elements of democracy as defined by the United Nations (1948), listed here in abbreviated form:

- respect for human rights and fundamental freedoms

TABLE 2.1
Democratic Governance Measures

Category/Construct	Description	At Multiple Time Points	By Country	By U.S. State	By U.S. County or City	By Subgroup	Raw Data Available for Research
				Data Availability			
Holding of periodic free and fair elections	**Source:** National Conference of State Legislatures (NCSL), 2022b **What is tracked:** A large variety of election law and procedural processes, including absentee voting, alternative voting methods, voter ID and registration, election security, and more	X		X			X
Respect for human rights and fundamental freedoms	**Source:** Human Rights Campaign and Equality Federation Institute (HRC&EF), 2022 **What is tracked:** Statewide laws and policies that affect LBGTQ+ people and their families	X		X			
Relates to all aspects of our definition of democracy	**Source:** Freedom House, undated-e **What is tracked:** Degree of democratic governance, as reflected by Global Freedom rating capturing a variety of information about political rights and civil liberties	X	X				X
Respect for human rights and fundamental freedoms	**Source:** Bloomberg Law, 2021 **What is tracked:** State provisions related to disability protections			X			

Table 2.1—Continued

Category/Construct	Description	Data Availability					
		At Multiple Time Points	By Country	By U.S. State	By U.S. County or City	By Subgroup	Raw Data Available for Research
The separation of powers and independence of the judiciary	**Source:** Organisation for Economic Co-Operation and Development (OECD), 2021b **What is tracked:** Citizen access to justice	X	X				X
Transparency and accountability in public administration; access to power and its exercise in accordance with rule of law	**Source:** Transparency International, 2021 **What is tracked:** Perceptions of public sector corruption	X	X				X
A pluralistic system of political parties and organizations	**Source:** OECD, 2021b **What is tracked:** Demographic composition in government and elected positions	X	X			X	X
	Source: NCSL, 2020 **What is tracked:** Demographic composition of state legislatures	X		X		X	
	Source: Schaefer, 2021b **What is tracked:** Demographic composition of federal legislature	X				X	

NOTE: LBGTQ+ = lesbian, gay, bisexual, transgender and queer plus people who use different language to describe identity (HRC&EF, 2022).

- rule of law
- free and fair elections
- a pluralistic system of political parties and organizations
- separation of powers and independence of judiciary
- transparency and accountability in public administration
- free, independent, and pluralistic media.

What is and is not captured through democratic governance measures. The first column of Table 2.1 provides information about how each measure we identified aligns with this definition. Broadly speaking, these measures fell into three categories: laws or policies; access or participation; and representation or action. Freedom House's measure of Global Freedom is the most comprehensive and contains measures that are related to every one of the essential elements of democracy we identified. The OECD and Transparency International also provide useful data on how the United States scores on measures of political rights, civil liberties, control of corruption, rule of law, and other related areas in comparison with other countries. Although comprehensive data on democratic governance is available on a country-by-country basis via Freedom House, OECD, and Transparency International, ratings on the extent of democratic governance are not generally available on a state-by-state basis in the United States, which could make sense given the wide variation in laws and policies across states. We identified a few exceptions to that rule that specifically examine state laws and policies reflecting human rights and fundamental freedoms for particular groups of people. HRC&EF (2022), for example, include an equality index of state legislation affecting the LGBTQ+ community. We also identified a study from Bloomberg Law (2021) detailing state-by-state provisions related to disability protection. These are the only items we found that measure state legislation related to vulnerable, minoritized, or protected populations. Although the National Womens Law Center (undated), as one example, identifies wage and poverty gaps for women versus men by state, it does not identify the specific legislation on a state-by-state basis that differentially affects women. The NCSL also released a brief (Salazar, 2016) examining the number of states that officially recognize American Indian tribes but did not provide any state-by-state data in that regard.

Furthermore, although we have state-by-state measures for diverse representation in the legislative branch and some idea of how representation in U.S. government institutions compares with other countries, we lack measures of representativeness at the county or local government level.

The NCSL provides data on a large variety of voting-related laws and policies state by state, from roundups of state laws for showing identification at the polls to those governing permissions for absentee and mail-in voting. The NCSL also provides data on redistricting laws and representation in governance, both of which provide some information about laws that can affect equity in access and representation. NCSL summarizes laws in a variety of ways, including both in text and databases, although researchers would need to code or organize the data themselves to conduct any quantitative analyses.

Signals that these measures provide about civic infrastructure. We scanned all of our identified measures to consider what they suggest regarding trends in democratic governance in the United States. This scan suggests the following three trends, which we describe in greater detail in the paragraphs that follow:

- The strength of U.S. democratic institutions and their transparency has been declining in recent years.
- State legislatures have enacted a considerable amount of legislation related to individual political rights and civil liberties in the past few years. However, there is a diverging pattern here; some states have restricted rights, while other states have expanded them.
- Congressional representatives have become gradually more diverse; nevertheless, there remain smaller populations of women and people under the age of 40 in many governmental and political positions in the United States at both the state and federal level.

Freedom House's most recent annual report indicated that U.S. democratic institutions have eroded in recent years (Freedom House, undated-e). This report gave U.S. political rights 32 out of 40 points and civil liberties 51 out of 60 points, which were both the same in 2021 but down from 2020. The evidence that Freedom House cited for its ratings of the United States included antidemocratic actions of January 6, 2021; laws that have made voting more difficult; and restrictions limiting discussion of topics related to race or gender in public school and university settings. In 2021, Transparency International similarly rated corruption in the United States to be at its highest since 2012, noting exploitation associated with the rapid rollout of the CARES pandemic relief package, attacks on whistleblowers during the Trump administration, and lack of oversight over money laundering activities (Burkhart, 2021). Both Freedom House and Transparency International have rated the United States lower than numerous other democratic nations, including the United Kingdom, Germany, France, Australia, Canada, and Japan.

NCSL data provides the greatest in-depth data on state laws related to elections and redistricting, among other topics. The laws governing elections are remarkably complex, vary across states, and include procedural issues that include absentee and mail-in voting, canvassing, certification and contested election deadlines, early voting, election observers and poll watchers, voting rights for felons, poll workers, primary voting processes, provisional ballots, recounts, voter ID laws, and countless others. NCSL noted that an "astounding 3,676 election bills were introduced" over the course of 2021, the highest number over the past 20 years, partially because of the larger demand for absentee or mail ballots during the pandemic and corresponding concerns voiced about the legitimacy of such methods (NCSL, 2022a). The largest portion of bills focused on ballot drop boxes and limits on ballot collection, including more security requirements for drop boxes and stipulations for numbers of drop boxes. Several states expanded automatic voter registration and mail-in voting, although at least one state repealed its Election Day registration law and several states added voter identification requirements to absentee ballot requests or returns.

Redistricting is another area where states vary considerably and where a large amount of legislation has been passed in recent years. Key differences among states include whether the state legislature or a redistricting committee has the power to redraw district lines; whether public input into the redistricting process is mandatory, optional, or pursued at all; the number of votes required to redraw district maps; and how challenges to redistricting maps are handled (NCSL, 2021).

Looking at state-by-state measures of rights for protected classes of individuals, an HRC&EF (2022) index indicates that state laws and policies supporting rights of LBGTQ+ individuals have also proliferated over the past several years, with 44 laws passed in 2021 that support LBGTQ+ parenting and nondiscrimination and sanction hate crimes. On the other hand, 27 bills signed into law in 2021 limited LBGTQ+ rights, including those preventing transgender youth from playing school sports consistent with their gender identity or receiving gender-affirming health care. In addition, more than 40 states have considered or passed legislation that limits schools from using curriculum or topics that address gender identity or sexual orientation (Jones and Franklin, 2022; Schwartz, 2022). As noted by Bloomberg Law (2021), most states require that businesses provide reasonable accommodations for people with disabilities, unless employers can demonstrate that these accommodations would impose undue hardships on them. However, Bloomberg Law (2021) also reports that three states—Alabama, Arkansas, and Florida—have no state statutory or regulatory provisions that apply to private-sector employment for people with disabilities.

The NCLS, the OECD, and the Pew Research Center have also tracked the demographic composition of state and federal legislatures, among other public service positions. As the Pew Research Center has noted, the House of Representatives and the Senate are the most diverse they have ever been racially, ethnically, and by gender, although Congress remains less diverse than the U.S. population (Schaeffer, 2021a). In terms of representation of women in public-sector and governmental employment, the United States is roughly on par with the average across other OECD country but lower than such countries as Sweden, Australia, Canada, and Great Britain (OECD, 2021b). These data also demonstrate that the composition of the U.S. Congress was markedly older than that of nearly any other OECD country in 2020, with the exception of France; the U.S. Cabinet was also older in average age than every OECD country except Japan and South Korea (OECD, 2021b).

Civic Education

Civic education is an input that we would likely expect to have the most impact on our output of civic literacy, given that civic education encompasses opportunities that individuals have to grow in their civic literacy and hone their civic identity and dispositions. These inputs include such things as academic standards and requirements governing civic education and informal (for example, outside classrooms) and formal civic learning opportunities in K–12 and higher education settings or beyond (Table 2.2).

What is and is not captured in the United States through civic education measures. As noted in Table 2.2, several studies have provided evidence of state policies on the minimum requirements that students must meet to graduate, as well as the content of state social studies standards. Such studies are not measuring formal civic learning opportunities directly; instead, they are measuring the standards and requirements that could influence those opportunities.

Although we thus know a fair amount about variation in state policies related to civic education, we know much less about what civic instruction looks like in K–12 classrooms and schools. We would particularly benefit from more-comprehensive data on the civic learning course and graduation requirements, as well as on civic-related electives available, at the school or district level across the United States. These data would be particularly helpful for understanding disparities in civic learning opportunities. In addition, data on civic education policies are fast becoming outdated (most research occurred in 2018, coinciding with the administration of the National Assessment of Educational Progress [NAEP] Civics Assessment) and do not reflect change over time that would be valuable for understanding whether civic education policies are proliferating. Lastly, we have no clear data on informal civic learning opportunities or postsecondary opportunities provided through higher education or in other settings.

Signals that these measures provide about civic infrastructure. The most-comprehensive measures we found for civic education are mostly state-level measures focused on academic standards and course requirements for civic education. These data indicate some areas of continuity across the United States regarding what is taught. Nearly all states have incorporated similar requirements for civic education within their academic standards— for example, at least some emphasis on current events and media literacy. As of 2017, nearly one-half of states had adopted a framework from National Council for the Social Studies (2013) that was developed through a collaboration among 15 professional organizations committed to the advancement of social studies education (Hansen et al., 2018). This framework provides guidance on the inquiry-based methods through which students can

TABLE 2.2

Civic Education Measures

Category/ Construct	Description	Data Availability					
		At Multiple Time Points	By Country	By U.S. State	By U.S. County or City	By Subgroup	Raw Data Available to Researchers
Laws or policies governing civic education	**Source:** Hansen et al., 2018 **What is tracked:** K–12 course requirements for civics and civics topics covered			X			
	Source: Stern et al., 2021 **What is tracked:** Ratings for K–12 state academic standards in civics and U.S. history			X			
	Source: Media Literacy Now, 2020 **What is tracked:** K–12 media literacy standards			X			
	Source: Shapiro and Brown, 2018 **What is tracked:** Civics education requirements (for example, courses, curriculum, community service, exams)			X			
	Source: Schwartz, 2022; Stout and Wilburn, 2022 **What is tracked:** Legislative efforts to restrict and expand education on racism, bias, the contributions of specific racial or ethnic groups to U.S. history			X			
Formal civic learning opportunities	**Source:** Hamilton, Kaufman, and Hu, 2020 **What is tracked:** K–12 students' participation in various civic learning opportunities, according to teacher self-report					X	

acquire key social studies content, and it specifically calls for students to draw on social studies disciplinary knowledge to develop questions, apply disciplinary content and tools, use evidence, and work collaboratively with other students (National Council for the Social Studies, 2013). Yet, the C3 framework is agnostic regarding the content of instruction (Herczog, 2013).

Ratings and reviews of policy and requirements for civic education note considerable areas of difference and inadequacy as well. For example, Stern et al. (2021) gave 35 states either a "mediocre" or "inadequate" rating for their K–12 history or civics standards, and the requirements for the extent of media literacy and civic education instruction are weak in most states (Media Literacy Now, undated; Shapiro and Brown, 2018). Furthermore, states vary considerably in their recent policies regarding what can and cannot be taught in classrooms regarding gender and race (Stout and Wilburn, 2022); 17 states have already passed formal legislation to limit discussions of these topics in the classroom (Schwartz, 2022).

We have not identified any systematic data at the state level or at a finer-grained level that provide information regarding students' civic learning opportunities in schools. Thus, although we know something about the requirements or standards that schools are expected to strive for, we do not know the extent to which schools are actually teaching critical topics in civic education and the types of civic courses and requirements to which students may be exposed. That said, as noted by Hamilton, Kaufman, and Hu (2020), we do know that the types of civic instructional approaches and topics that students are exposed to—at least based on teacher self-report—vary according to student grade level, school poverty level and urbanicity, teacher ethnicity, and several other factors that differ across and within states. For example, secondary teachers reported that they emphasized discussions of current events and knowledge of the political system while elementary teachers reported more emphasis on developing students' social and emotional skills (Hamilton, Kaufman, and Hu, 2020).

Taken together, these data suggest that a given student will receive considerably different civic education instruction depending on where they live, the type of school they attend, and who their teachers are.

Civic Spaces

To facilitate civic discourse, there must be equitable physical and virtual spaces in which individuals can engage in civic discourse and participate in civic activities. Measures of civic spaces would therefore ideally capture not just access to these spaces and the extent to which they allow for equitable participation, but the actual degree and nature of such participation, as well as how laws or policies support that participation (Table 2.3).

What is and is not captured in the United States through civic spaces measures. Measures that match our criteria focus mainly on access to open civic spaces (newspaper deserts, access to either broadband internet or physical spaces in the communities). Tracking broadband internet access (a proxy for virtual civic space) and access to physical spaces in the community, such as parks and libraries, are a minimal way to monitor whether the built environment provides areas that can potentially serve as civic spaces.

The access measures we identified represent both virtual and physical realms, but more is needed to adequately represent each of them. For example, in the physical realm, parks and libraries are not the only public (and nonpublic) spaces that might support civic engagement, and ideal measures would capture other physical spaces that facilitate civic discourse, such as community centers, arenas, auditoriums, etc. Although Reimagining the Civic Commons (undated-b) has released baseline and follow up metrics related to how physical spaces support public life, those metrics are available for only four cities where investments are being monitored: Akron, Ohio; Chicago, Illinois; Detroit, Michigan; and Memphis, Tennessee. The Public Library Survey data from the Institute of Museum and Library Services provides more-detailed data on public libraries, including the number and percentage distribution of public libraries by state, by size of population, and by other metrics, such as public service hours (Pelczar et al., 2021).

Furthermore, metrics often describe presence of potential civic spaces (for example, access to broadband, parks, libraries) rather than use or participation in those civic spaces. Reimagining the Civic Commons is one exception in terms of measuring many aspects of use of civic spaces, although those metrics are available in only a few cities. The Public Library Survey also provides data on visits to public libraries (Pelczar et al., 2021).

The measures we identified do a fair job of monitoring differences in the existence of some civic spaces across geographic regions and capturing sub-

TABLE 2.3

Civic Spaces Measures

Category/Construct	Description	Data Availability					
		At Multiple Time Points	By Country	By U.S. State	By U.S. County or City	By Subgroup	Raw Data Available to Researchers
Laws governing civic spaces	**Source:** Freedom House, undated-d **What is tracked:** Internet freedom	X	X				X
Access to virtual or physical open spaces	**Source:** Federal Communications Commission, undated; Martin, 2021; OECD, 2021a; Pew Research Center, 2021a **What is tracked:** Internet access	X	X	X	X	X	X
	Source: Trust for Public Land, undated **What is tracked:** Access to parks	X			X	X	
	Source: University of North Carolina Hussman School of Journalism and Media, undated **What is tracked:** Newspaper deserts	X		X	X		
Both access to and use of open spaces	**Source:** Institute of Museum and Library Services, undated **What is tracked:** Access to public libraries and their use	X		X			X
	Source: Reimagining the Civic Commons, undated-a **What is tracked:** Access to and participation in civic spaces	X			X		
Public use of virtual open spaces	**Source:** Rideout et al., 2022 **What is tracked:** Social media use among tweens and teens	X				X	

national differences. However, not as many measures we identified provide clear, systematic information on intrastate differences beyond civic spaces measures (for example, internet access, newspaper deserts).

Signals that these measures provide about civic infrastructure. The United States is generally regarded as one of the freer countries in terms of internet freedom (one potential measure that could be used as a proxy for the extent of virtual civic spaces), although its score in 2021 was lower than that of 11 other countries, including Iceland, Estonia, Canada, Costa Rica, Germany, France, and Taiwan. The United States' internet freedom score—and that of many countries—has declined over the past five years because of proliferation of misinformation. At the same time, as noted by Freedom House (undated-d), the United States' "laissez-faire approach to the tech industry created opportunities for authoritarian manipulation, data exploitation, and widespread malfeasance."

Even in this internet-based era, 15 percent of households still lack broadband internet access (Martin, 2021). More concerningly, lack of broadband access is concentrated among Black households, those making less than $25,000 per year, and those in rural areas. Similarly, the number of counties that are newspaper deserts is growing, reaching more than 200 in 2020. Increasingly, those areas without local newspapers tend to be isolated and economically vulnerable (Abernathy, 2020).

Impressively, 97 percent of people within a given geographical area live within the service area of one of America's 17,278 public library outlets, and 37 states report that one-half or more of the people living in a given library service area had a library card as of fiscal year 2019 (Pelczar et al., 2021). That said, library usage is also likely related to the variety of staff and resources available at a given library. The COVID-19 pandemic, particularly, has shed light on the important need for internet access across virtual spaces, at the same time that researchers have tracked an increase in use of social media by tweens and teens during the pandemic, which could affect their socialization and well-being (Rideout and Robb, 2021).

The gaps in internet access, library access, and newspaper deserts across the United States make clear that many people lack access to virtual and civic spaces. This lack of access likely results in lower civic literacy, identity, and engagement in many U.S. communities, as well as lower trust in governance (Sullivan, 2021).

Outputs

As noted in the previous chapter, we define civic literacy as civic knowledge and skills. Civic identity encompasses a wider variety of individual and group beliefs and dispositions, from political affiliation to feelings of civic duty and pride to social responsibility. Lastly, civic engagement is meant to capture various types of political and social participation, from community service to political activities and participation in events, such as protests and other activities that may drive social change. In this section, we list measures associated with each of these outputs that meet our baseline content and reliability/validity criteria, as well as at least one other of the criteria we have used to judge quality of measures: comparability over time, geographical areas, or subgroups.

Civic Literacy

Measures of civic literacy should capture whether people of all ages have obtained the foundational civic knowledge (for example, how the government works, rights protected by the Constitution) and skills (for example, critical thinking skills to examine and question biases in published works) through their formal and informal education to meaningfully engage in civic life. Thus, our measures of civic literacy focus on a single critical construct (civic knowledge and skills) that we expect could have broad impact on civic outcomes across the United States (Table 2.4).

What is and is not captured in the United States through civic literacy measures. Results from standardized assessments are the best available proxy for directly measuring both students' and adults' civic knowledge and skills. The NAEP Civics Assessment provides regular monitoring of U.S. students' proficiency in civics, although the most-recent assessments have only focused on the middle school (grade 8) level. The assessment is specifically "designed to measure the civics knowledge and skills that are critical to the responsibilities of citizenship in the constitutional democracy of the United States" (NAEP, 2021). NAEP also includes assessments in other social studies subjects (for example, U.S. history, economics, geography) that also might contribute to developing students' civic literacy.

TABLE 2.4
Civic Literacy Measures

Category/Construct	Description	Data Availability					
		At Multiple Time Points	By Country	By U.S. State	By U.S. County or City	By Subgroup	Raw Data Available to Researchers
Civic knowledge/skills	**Source:** NAEP, 2021 **What is tracked:** Student proficiency in grades 4, 8, and 12 on a national civics assessment	X				X	X
	Source: Annenberg Public Policy Center, undated **What is tracked:** U.S adults' knowledge of the Constitution and how government works	X					
	Source: OECD, 2021a **What is tracked:** Proficiency in distinguishing facts from opinions among 15-year-olds		X			X	X
Broad knowledge/skills	**Source:** Programme for the International Assessment of Adult Competencies, undated **What is tracked:** Proficiency in literacy and numeracy skills among all adults ages 16–74	X	X	X	X	X	X

Furthermore, the College Board administers annual "Advanced Placement" exams to high-school students, including one specifically focused on U.S. government and politics. This exam assesses college-level proficiency in this content area; because students self-select into taking the exam, participation in this exam also provides some indication of students' disposition to do advanced coursework in civics. Together, these measures provide strong national evidence of students' civic knowledge as they progress through and exit the formal education system. Such civic skills as students' critical thinking and communication skills, however, are not necessarily measured by these tests and courses.

Monitoring of civic knowledge and skills is essential, even after departure from the formal education system, because presumably some of the civic knowledge and skills that adults gained in the formal education system fades over time. The Annenberg Public Policy Center at the University of Pennsylvania attempts to address this gap by conducting an annual survey of U.S. adults that asks respondents to recall basic facts about how the government functions. Meanwhile, the Programme for International Assessment of Adult Competencies (undated) captures adults' literacy and numeracy skills more generally, although this assessment is not specific to civic knowledge. However, we consider this an important indicator of civic literacy because proficiency in literacy and numeracy generally are important indicators of adults' skills in performing activities that we expect would be directly related to civic discourse and civic engagement, such as reading the newspaper, critically examining arguments, and understanding and interpreting written text and figures.

Although there is some monitoring of students' proficiency in civics while they are in the formal K–12 education system (including through NAEP and other state standardized assessments), there are no systematic data at the state level allowing for comparisons about civic literacy among students in different states. Furthermore, the fact that the United States has not participated in the international civic assessment (International Association for the Evaluation of Educational Achievement, undated) since 1999 makes it virtually impossible to monitor how U.S. students' civic knowledge and skills compare with their international peers.

Although the Annenberg Public Policy Center's annual Civic Knowledge Survey provides some evidence of adults' civic knowledge, data are not available at the state level, and there are limited data by subgroup. Furthermore, although this annual survey tells us something about adults' knowledge of how government works on paper, it cannot tell us about adults' knowledge of how government operates in practice and how policy is typically proposed, adopted, and implemented across geographic levels.

Signals that these measures provide about civic infrastructure. Although we lack state-by-state measures of civic knowledge and skills, NAEP provides at least a national picture of civics knowledge. That picture is not reassuring: Just under one-quarter of students scored at or above proficient in civics with a 20-point gap between white students and their Black or Hispanic peers (Nation's Report Card, undated-a). In general, NAEP scores have been mostly the same, increasing only slightly since 1998.

In terms of proficiency in distinguishing facts from opinions—a skill indicative of both civic and media literacy—an estimated 80 percent of 15-year-old students in the United States receive training on how to recognize bias in information, a percentage far higher than in other countries. U.S. students also performed above average on an international assessment examining their ability to distinguish facts from opinions (OECD, 2021a).

Interestingly, civic literacy among U.S. adults appears to be increasing. The Annenberg Civics Knowledge Survey indicates that, in 2021, more Americans could name all three branches of government and rights protected by the First Amendment than could in prior years (Annenberg Public Policy Center, 2021). Americans' civic literacy is, of course, likely connected to their overall literacy, which—according to recent assessments by the National Center for Education Statistics (NCES)—did not shift demonstrably between 2014 and 2017. Specifically, nearly 20 percent of U.S. adults performed at the lowest levels in literacy, and nearly 30 percent did so in numeracy (NCES, undated-a).

Civic Identity

We looked for measures of civic identity that reflected our definition, which regards civic identity as encompassing (1) attitudes toward political participation, including political self-efficacy, trust in governance, and political leaning; (2) feelings of civic or social duty and responsibility, and (3) sense of belonging within and pride regarding one's country, state, or community

(Table 2.5). As noted in our definition chapter, civic identity is intertwined with (but not the same as) individuals' sense of their own identity, given that the ways in which individuals identify may be related to political attitudes, civic and social responsibility, or sense of belonging in a particular place.

Like civic literacy, we expect that one's civic identity is cultivated in both formal and informal educational settings as well as through interpersonal interactions that occur over time. Ideally, measures related to civic identity would capture a wide variety of constructs that may be related to civic literacy and engagement, the other civic outcomes we have defined for this project, using research and theory.

What is and is not captured through civic identity measures. The measures available to track feelings of civic identity are generally public opinion polls that ask about individuals' beliefs and attitudes toward their community and civic life. For example, Gallup has been tracking since 2001 the share of the U.S. population that expresses pride in being an American. This semiregular public opinion poll also tracks what specific aspects of their country that Americans take pride in, such as scientific achievements, diversity, the political system, and the military. Similarly, ANES collects data on a wide variety of values and dispositions held by members of the U.S. electorate, including their perception of whether voting—likely the best available proxy for civic engagement—is a duty, their perception of whether they have a say in what government does (political efficacy), and their feelings of responsibility to build a society that works well for all people. There are also high-quality data on individuals' political and ideological preferences, captured by several organizations.

Although public opinion polling captures many of the attitudes and beliefs related to our constructs of interest, many public opinion polls are not conducted regularly enough to monitor many of these trends, and there are many limitations to public polling (for example, Foad et al., 2021; Rosenblatt, 1999). Even more importantly, although some of the measures do allow for some investigation of subgroup differences, measures do not capture subnational variation in civic identity. This is problematic, given likely variation across states and local communities in these measures. More measures are also needed to understand how peoples' feelings and attitudes toward their local community are similar to and different from their attitudes toward a national community.

TABLE 2.5

Civic Identity Measures

Category/ Construct	Description	Data Availability					
		At Multiple Time Points	By Country	By U.S. State	By U.S. County or City	By Subgroup	Raw Data Available to Researchers
Attitudes toward political participation	**Source:** Gallup, undated-a; Pew Research Center, undated; and Pew Research Center, 2020 **What is tracked:** Political party affiliation	X		X		X	X
	Source: American National Election Studies (ANES), undated-f **What is tracked:** Political ideology (liberal-conservative) self-identification	X				X	X
	Source: Gallup, undated-b; Jones, 2014; OECD, undated-b; Pew Research Center, 2022 **What is tracked:** Trust and confidence in government	X	X	X		X	X
	Source: ANES, undated-d **What is tracked:** Political efficacy index	X				X	X
Feelings of civic or social duty	**Source:** ANES, undated-a **What is tracked:** Extent to which people perceive voting as a civic duty versus a choice	X				X	X
Sense of belonging and pride	**Source:** Jones, 2021 **What is tracked:** Public opinion monitoring pride in being an American	X				X	

Signals that measures provide about civic infrastructure civic identity. Election studies from such groups as Gallup, ANES, and the Pew Research Center regularly poll U.S. adults on their political affiliation (that is, Democrat, Republican, independent) and ideological self-identification (that is, liberal or conservative). Gallup provides data on a monthly basis, and these data suggest ebbs and flows in whether respondents indicate leaning more Republican or Democrat, with respondents often (but not always) responding in slightly greater percentages that they lean Democrat rather than Republican. As noted by the Pew Research Center (2020), party identification has remained mostly the same among registered voters over the past several decades, although Democratic Party identification has dropped slightly since 2017. Those who identify as independent—or do not identify as Republican or Democrat—has also held relatively steady over the past several decades, although the number has risen slightly since about 2006. In general, party identification is heavily connected to individuals' demographic characteristics, including gender, race/ethnicity, and college education, among other factors (Pew Research Center, 2020).

Despite the relative stability of party identification, Americans' feelings of political efficacy have dropped in recent years. According to data from the ANES (undated-b), a little over 60 percent of Americans agreed with the statement, "People like me don't have any say about what the government does" in 2020, compared with 50 percent in 2016 and 44 percent in 2004.

Americans' declining positive views about what their government can do for them may also reflect low levels of national pride and trust in U.S. institutions. According to Gallup, U.S. national pride steadily dropped between 2004 and 2020, and trust in the federal government to handle domestic and international affairs was at some of its lowest levels by 2021 (Newport, 2022). U.S adults' trust in the national government is lower than in roughly one-half of OECD countries (OECD, undated) and trust in state governments varied substantially from state to state when it was measured back in 2014 (Jones, 2014). With respect to confidence in other U.S. institutions, minorities of Americans felt confidence in such institutions as the Supreme Court, the public school system, the criminal justice system, the President, and Congress in 2021, with confidence in those institutions dropping somewhat since 2020 (Brenan, 2021).

That said, national pride saw a small uptick in 2021 Gallup polls asking, "How proud are you to be an American?" Specifically, although 91 percent of Americans indicated being "very" or "extremely" proud to be Americans in 2004, that percentage dropped to 81 percent in 2016 and to an all-time low of 63 percent in 2020. But, it rebounded in 2021 to 69 percent (Jones, 2021). Similarly, the Pew Research Center (2022) identified a small uptick in public trust in 2021, particularly among Black Americans.

Civic Engagement

Our final output, civic engagement, encompasses three key constructs, which draw on Keeter et al., (2002) and Ekman and Amnå (2012), as noted in our definition chapter: (1) community service, (2) political participation and involvement, and (3) activities to drive social changes. The measures that we have listed in Table 2.6 are ones that we identified that both align with these content criteria and have validity evidence in more than one category included in our criteria.

What is and is not captured comprehensively across the United States through civic engagement measures? The measures available to track civic engagement are generally regular federal and nonfederal surveys that ask about individuals' political participation and involvement. For example, ANES collects data on a wide variety of civic engagement activities, such as contributing financially to political campaigns and attending political events. The U.S. Census Bureau's Current Population Survey's annual Volunteering and Civic Life Supplement provides data on the hours that individuals spend volunteering in the community and participating in political activities, such as attending protests and contacting public officials. The U.S. Census Bureau also collects state-level data on what most people typically consider the most common measure of civic engagement: voter registration and participation. These data are also collected regularly and at subnational levels by state election offices. Although multiple measures track electoral activities and activities intended to drive social and political change, the only measure of community service we found was the aforementioned U.S. Census Bureau measure of volunteering across the United States.

As noted, there are some high-quality data available on civic engagement activities collected through regular federal and nonfederal surveys. How-

TABLE 2.6

Civic Engagement Measures

Category/ Construct	Description	Data Availability					
		At Multiple Time Points	By Country	By U.S. State	By U.S. County or City	By Subgroup	Raw Data Available to Researchers
Community service activities	**Source:** U.S. Census Bureau, 2019 **What is tracked:** Percentage of individuals who indicated that they volunteered at an organization or association	X		X		X	X
Electoral activities	**Source:** U.S. Census Bureau, 2021a **What is tracked:** Proportion of individuals who are registered to vote among the eligible voting population	X		X		X	X
	Source: United States Election Project, undated; U.S. Census Bureau, 2021a; OECD Better Life Index, undated **What is tracked:** Voter turnout for elections	X	X	X	X	X	X
Activities to drive political and social change	**Source:** ANES, undated-e **What is tracked:** Percentage of individuals who financially supported a political campaign	X				X	X
	Source: ANES, undated-c **What is tracked:** Percentage of individuals who indicated that they attended a political event	X				X	X

Table 2.6—Continued

Category/Construct	Description	Data Availability					
		At Multiple Time Points	By Country	By U.S. State	By U.S. County or City	By Subgroup	Raw Data Available to Researchers
Activities to drive political and social change	**Source:** ANES, undated-a **What is tracked:** Percentage of individuals who indicated that they participated in a protest, march, or demonstration	X				X	X
	Source: Armed Conflict Location and Event Data Project, 2020; Bridging Divides Initiative at Princeton, undated **What is tracked:** Political demonstrations and political violence				X	X	
	Source: U.S. Census Bureau, 2019 **What is tracked:** Percentage of individuals who indicated that they contacted a public official at any level of government	X		X		X	X
	Source: U.S. Census Bureau, 2019 **What is tracked:** Frequency of discussing political, societal, or local issues with family, friends, and neighbors	X		X		X	X
	Source: U.S. Census Bureau, 2019 **What is tracked:** Frequency of posting views about political, societal, or local issues on social media	X		X		X	X

ever, many of these data collections happen only every few years or during election cycles. Even more importantly, although some of the measures do allow for some investigation of subgroup and state-level differences, there is very little systematic information available at the local community level. Although states do collect voting data at very fine grain levels, for example, these data are not easily accessible and vary in the degree to which they are disaggregated by demographics. This is problematic because we believe that there is likely great variation across local communities in these civic engagement measures, which may be indicative of systematic problems in equitable access to civic infrastructure.

We did not identify measures for any other activities that constitute civic engagement, such as serving on a jury, paying taxes, or serving as a poll worker during elections. These civic engagement activities, although critical to the health of our civic infrastructure, are not captured sufficiently in data collections.

What signals do these measures provide about civic infrastructure? Many of the measures we identified provide data about voter turnout. In general, voting turnout in the United States is lower than in many other democratic nations (OECD Better Life Index, undated). That said, voting turnout for the 2020 presidential election was the highest it had been since 1904, and midterm election turnout in 2018 was the highest since 1914, according to data drawn from the United States Election Project (FairVote, undated). Voter registration and turnout varies considerably by state and by certain demographics. For example, although only 52 percent of U.S. citizens in Arkansas voted in the November election, 78 percent did so in New Jersey. Although about 73 percent of citizens ages 65 to 74 voted in the November election, only 50 percent of 18- to 24-year-olds did so (U.S. Census Bureau, 2021a).

Contributions to political campaigns have grown somewhat over the past few decades. About 20 percent of Americans indicated that they gave money to a political campaign in 2020 versus less than 10 percent between the years of 1980 and 2000 (ANES, undated-e). Political protests in response to the murder of George Floyd and other high-profile police violence against Black Americans surged in 2020 (although they dropped following their high point in late May 2020) (Armed Conflict Location & Event Data Project, 2020).

According to analyses of U.S. Census Bureau data on volunteering (Schlachter, 2021), the rate of organization-based volunteering has remained relatively stable over time: About 30 percent of Americans have indicated volunteering for an organization. That said, volunteering varies widely by education level and somewhat by ethnicity, with those holding college degrees being much more likely to volunteer.

Measure Availability Across Civic Infrastructure Inputs and Outputs

Table 2.7 summarizes the availability of measures for the constructs encompassing our definitions for the inputs and outputs in our civic infrastructure framework. Again, readers should keep in mind that the measures we have identified are ones that addressed at least one of our comparative criteria. We may have overlooked some measures and not identified measures that address some of our inputs or outputs in ways that we did not define. Nevertheless, the measure availability summarized in Table 2.7 does suggest areas where we have better or worse coverage of civic infrastructure, as we have defined it. In the table, we categorized measure constructs and then indicated the extent of measurement sources on that topic, as well as coverage across our comparative criteria and data availability.

As can be noted in Table 2.7, we identified measures across the greatest number of criteria for constructs related to civic engagement: electoral activities and activities to drive political and social change. This is perhaps not surprising given that these constructs are commonly referenced to discuss or gauge aspects of civic infrastructure. That said, we found only one robust measure of volunteerism or community service. Relatedly, our civic identity measures captured attitudes toward political participation and political leaning far more than feelings of civic duty, responsibility, or pride.

For democratic governance, we have strong measurement sources internationally but fewer that capture data at the state level and none at the county or city level. Measures of democratic governance often cover more than one time point, which gives us more ability to track aspects of that input more carefully over time, especially when comparing the United States with other countries.

TABLE 2.7

Availability of Measures for Civic Infrastructure Inputs and Outputs, by Major Criteria

Input or Output	Measure Construct	>1 Measure Source	>1 Timepoint	Comparative Criteria				Raw Data Accessible to Researchers
				By Country	By U.S. State	By U.S. City or County	By Subgroup	
Democratic governance	Respect for human rights and fundamental freedoms	X	X	X	X			X
	Rule of law	X	X	X				X
	Free and fair elections	X	X	X	X			X
	A pluralistic system of political parties and organizations	X	X	X	X		X	X
	Separation of powers and independence of judiciary		X	X				X
	Transparency and accountability in public administration	X	X	X				X
	Free, independent, and pluralistic media		X	X				X

Table 2.7—Continued

Input or Output	Measure Construct	> 1 Measure Source	> 1 Timepoint	By Country	By U.S. State	By U.S. City or County	By Subgroup	Raw Data Accessible to Researchers
Civic education	Laws governing civics education	X			X			X
	Formal civic learning opportunities						X	
Civic spaces	Laws governing civic spaces		X	X		X	X	X
	Access to virtual or physical open spaces with potential for civic activities	X	X	X	X	X	X	X
	Public use of virtual or physical open spaces	X	X	X	X	X	X	X
Civic literacy	K–12 civic knowledge and skills	X	X	X			X	X
	Adult civic knowledge and skills		X					
	Literacy and numeracy skills		X	X	X	X	X	X

Table 2.7—Continued

		Comparative Criteria						
Input or Output	Measure Construct	> 1 Measure Source	> 1 Timepoint	By Country	By U.S. State	By U.S. City or County	By Subgroup	Raw Data Accessible to Researchers
Civic identity	Political leaning	X			X		X	X
	Attitudes toward political participation (self-efficacy, trust)	X	X	X	X		X	X
	Feelings of social or civic duty/responsibility		X				X	X
	Sense of belonging/pride		X				X	
Civic engagement	Volunteerism or community service	X	X		X		X	X
	Electoral activities	X	X	X	X	X	X	X
	Activities to drive political and social change	X	X	X	X	X	X	X

Of all of our inputs, we have the least amount of data on civic education, particularly across multiple time points. And, although we have many periodic roundups of state policies related to civic education by state, we have little other state information on which to draw to understand how civic education varies across the United States. Relatedly, we lack data on civic literacy by state or even a way to compare civic literacy in the United States compared with other countries. Thus, we lack the information to know whether any activities undertaken in the United States potentially improve civic education and, as a result, civic literacy.

We identified rich data on civic spaces in terms of measures capturing equitable access to open spaces that might support civic discourse and purposes (the internet, parks, newspapers). However, we identified very few laws or policies to support civic spaces, in contrast with the many law/policy roundups related to civic education. We also did not identify many good measures of use of open, public spaces, although some do exist (for use of libraries across the United States and outdoor civic spaces in some small cities).

CHAPTER 3

Conclusion and Implications

We cannot know whether our American democracy is at risk if we lack definitions and measures on the strength of our civic infrastructure. Without these definitions, we cannot track changes to civic infrastructure over time, nor can we identify variation in the health of our civic infrastructure across the United States and the globe that might point to places and people to learn from or to areas that might need more resources for improvements.

This report offers a starting point for defining and measuring—along with monitoring change and variation in—U.S. civic infrastructure. We developed a framework for defining and measuring civic infrastructure through an extensive exploration of the literature, first delving into broader definitions of civic infrastructure and then into more fine-grained literature searches for key aspects of civic infrastructure we identified. Then, we conducted a comprehensive search of measures related to our framework, investigating both what is and is not captured through measures and what signals about civic infrastructure we can glean from those measures. We also sought input from a variety of scholars at the RAND Corporation and beyond to get input on our framework and measures.

Our framework begins with Blair and Koppell's (2015) definition of civic infrastructure as the "places, policies, programs, and practices" that undergird strong communities and foster civic engagement. We expand on that definition in terms of three key inputs: democratic governance, civic education, and civic spaces. Through these inputs, we hypothesize that three main outputs of civic infrastructure can be strengthened: civic literacy, civic identity, and civic engagement.

What Aspects of U.S. Civic Infrastructure That Align with Our Framework Are (and Are Not) Measured?

Aspects of civic infrastructure that are covered most comprehensively are those related to political participation. We identified a wide variety of measures addressing political participation, including those related to voting laws, political leanings, attitudes toward political participation, and voter registration and turnout. ANES, for example, tracks voter registration and voting each year, and it splits data by state and subgroup. The Volunteering and Civic Life Supplement of the Current Population Survey also captures percentages of individuals who contact a public official or volunteer year by year, across the country and states, and by subgroup. That said, many of those measures are not easily accessible, especially by state and subgroup, and are available only in data formats that require more analytic skill to examine.

Access to potential civic spaces are also captured through measures across numerous criteria, but often use a few very strong measures of only certain aspects of civic infrastructure. For example, internet access is captured across multiple time points, by country, by state, and at even finer-grained levels by various organizations. Similarly, access to public parks from the Trust for Public Land (undated) meets many of our criteria. That said, nearly all measures of civic spaces capture equitable access to civic spaces across geographies rather than examining laws, policies, or representation in civic spaces.

Measures provide some indication of international variation in democratic governance and transparency across countries, but state-by-state data and local data—a critical disaggregation given the federal nature of the U.S. system—are often lacking. Some of the most-comprehensive data regarding the state of democracy come from measures comparing the United States to other countries over time, including Freedom House and OECD measures. Transparency International similarly captures annual data on perceptions of public-sector corruption across 180 countries and territories. Freedom House and Transparency International methods and rubrics also provide a clear vision for aspects of democratic governance aligned with the ideals for civic infrastructure we identified. However, these types of data would also be valuable on a state-by-state basis, given differences in political rights and civil liberties across U.S. states. Although some reports examine laws reflecting political rights for particular protected classes (for example, LGBTQ+ communities, people with disabilities), we did not identify any state-by-state data on legislation that affects many other protected or vulnerable groups. Nor did we find reports that compare political rights or civil liberties across U.S. states. In addition, although the NCSL provides excellent state-by-state details on voting policies, redistricting rules, and much more, those data could be systematically organized and summarized in files that could be used more easily in analyses.

Input measures that provide some information about state-by-state variation focus more on state policies, laws, and access rather than actual participation. As we have noted at several points in this report, civic infrastructure inputs and outputs vary considerably depending on where one lives—particularly the state in which one lives. For that reason, state-by-state measures—as well as more measures that capture civic infrastructure at an even more fine-grained level, such as county—are likely critical to understanding civic infrastructure. We identified an array of state-by-state measures, including state measures related to the following inputs:

- democratic governance
  - electoral and redistricting rules
  - policies that affect the rights of LBGTQ+ people
  - demographic composition of state legislatures
- civic education
  - K–12 civics course requirements
  - topics covered by state academic standards for social studies and media literacy
  - laws limiting or expanding education on racism, gender, bias, and the contributions of specific racial or ethnic groups
  - educator diversity policies and data
- civic spaces
  - internet access
  - newspaper deserts.

Although these state-by-state data provide useful information about the diversity of state laws and requirements and about access to important civic spaces (such as the internet), they provide little to no insight regarding the extent of participation in various civic inputs. For example, to better understand equality in access and participation in civics education opportunities, we would ideally know what percentage of students took civics courses in high school at a state-by-state level (or even civic course participation more broadly across the United States and by student subgroup). We would also ideally know the extent to which students were able to participate in community service or other nontraditional civic learning opportunities on a state-by-state basis. We have the means to gather some of these data at the state level. For example, states report an array of data to the federal government and could also report civics course and community service participation data in some standardized way. Furthermore, intrastate data would likely demonstrate additional variation and places where civic infrastructure is particularly lacking. Throughout our analyses, we note the lack of finer-grained data that might allow for such analyses.

At the output level, very little comparative data at the state level provides any indication of students' civic literacy and Americans' civic identity in the United States. Although the International Civic and Citizenship Education Study provides some comparative country-by-country data, the United States has not participated in the study's civics assessments since 1999. NAEP periodically tests students' civic knowledge and skills, but that data is only available nationally and by subgroups for students in fourth and eighth grade. Funding to expand NAEP across states would at least give us some standardized idea of variation in students' civic literacy and where more investments in civic education could be useful. As noted, civic engagement data are captured more broadly across states through ANES, but that data is harder to access at a fine-grained level within states.

What Do The Measures Identified Say About the Strength of U.S. Civic Infrastructure?

The most-robust measures we have identified provide some indication of the strength of our civic infrastructure, although we did not conduct any formal analysis for this report and—particularly—did not look at associations between the civic infrastructure inputs and the outputs in our framework. However, looking across the measures in our framework provides useful information on trends.

Both input and output data suggest a downturn in many measures of democratic governance over the past several years, although some civic engagement measures have ticked slightly upward in the past year or so. International measures of multiple aspects of democracy have reported lower scores for the United States over the past several years. Freedom House's ratings of U.S. political rights and civil rights, as well as internet freedoms, have been steadily declining over the past several years while Transparency International's ratings of corruption in the United States have been rising. In addition, Americans' feelings of political efficacy—an output we tie to our civic identity output—has been declining precipitously over the past several years. Furthermore, although the United States is generally regarded as more democratic and freer than many other countries, multiple countries around the globe are rated higher than the United States on these measures, including Argentina, Canada, France, Germany, Latvia, Mongolia, and the United Kingdom.

At the same time, other civic outcome measures have slightly increased or remained steady, including measures of adults' knowledge of government, along with rates of voter turnout and political protest.

In the past several years, there has been a proliferation of state legislation focused on changing individual rights. However, there is a diverging pattern: Some states are restricting Americans' civil and political rights; other states are expanding them. Over the past few years, some of our measures reflect a proliferation of contrasting state legislation. For example, in 2021, the number of election bills introduced in state legislatures was at its highest rate in decades (NCSL, 2022a), with bills both restricting and expanding voter rights. Similarly, HRC&EF (2022) tracked over 70 laws in 2021 that either expanded or limited LBGTQ+ rights. Lastly, in the past year, numerous states have passed or are considering bills to restrict education on racism, bias, and the contributions of specific racial and ethnic groups to U.S. history, although multiple states have also passed bills expanding such education (Stout and Wilburn, 2022). The growing number of states passing restrictions or expansions of rights makes clear that individual political and civil rights and freedoms look quite different for people depending on the state in which they live. Thus, for example, a person living in a state with more-restrictive voting laws, more limits on LBGTQ+ rights, and more limits on discussions of race and ethnicity in the classroom will have access to different civic opportunities than a counterpart in a different state with more rights and freedoms.

Relatedly, state-by-state variation across many of our civic input and output measures suggests unequal access to the opportunities that drive civic literacy, identity, and engagement in the United States. Where state measures exist, they illustrate the considerable variation in civic inputs and outputs that we tracked, including measures for access to parks and newspapers, as well as civic engagement measures, such as those that capture voter registration and turnout. Although we lack state-by-state measures in other critical areas, such measures would likely tell the same story: The state in which a person lives—and even the county—likely determines much about that person's civic infrastructure and, thus, the factors driving civic outputs.

Diversity of our population is expanding, and yet we lack diversity in critical areas of civic infrastructure. As the U.S. population becomes more ethnically diverse, our measures have captured some growing diversity in other areas, such as diversity of our congressional representatives (Schaeffer, 2021b). Thus, although the U.S. population is diverse by gender, age, socioeconomic status, and education level (among other factors), U.S. governing institutions do not reflect these wide-ranging experiences. For example, international data sources suggest that the average age of cabinet and congressional representatives at the federal level is much older than in other countries (OECD, 2021a). We lack data on the diversity of representation in civic spaces, which could point to ways that we might strengthen diversity in that area.

What Are the Limitations of This Research?

This exploratory research has several limitations. First, although it presents a framework for civic infrastructure that is derived from considerable research on the factors that drive civic outcomes, the only validity evidence presented in this report for our framework comes from literature review and guidance from experts. We have not, for example, conducted any quantitative analysis examining relationships among our proposed civic infrastructure inputs and outputs, although we have reviewed literature that does. In addition, although we have identified multiple measures aligned with our civic infrastructure framework as examples, there are likely additional measures that might meet our criteria.

Second, we identified several criteria for measures that we included in the second chapter of this report. In almost all cases, even when measures met some criteria, they typically did not meet all criteria and were not ideal measures for multiple other reasons (for example, they were not easily accessible, not part of formal datasets that could be merged with other data, or not available at multiple geographic levels). In addition, those criteria may have limited us from providing examples of some potentially useful measures that are only available at one time point, for example, or for one geographical area. Thus, the measures we have presented should very much be regarded only as examples and not necessarily high-quality models or the best way to measure a given construct.

Lastly, our framework and measures for civic infrastructure are specifically derived from conceptions and theories of democracy in general and Western democracy in particular. Thus, although our proposed measures and the ideals undergirding them may provide guidance on how civic infrastructure could drive civic outcomes in a democratic nation, those measures may be of limited usefulness in nondemocratic settings. That said, our framework and measures could be useful in contexts or countries that purport to be democratic but provide weak evidence of a strong civic infrastructure. In cases where our measures reflect a weak civic infrastructure, we hypothesize weak support for a functioning democracy.

What Are the Implications and Next Steps for This Research?

Implications for research. Given the exploratory nature of this study, much more research is necessary to test and confirm our framework and measures. This research could include gathering more validity evidence to both identify the best measures reflecting the constructs we have created and to test relationships among constructs in our framework. Researchers can also contribute by helping figure out how to bring some comprehensive data together in a meaningful way. For example, research could identify existing scales and develop new ones that would provide optimal evidence about the constructs we identified and test those measures in various ways through qualitative data (for example, validity evidence related to response processes for self-report scales) and quantitative data (for example, internal structure of scales and relationships to other variables). In addition, although Chapter 1 provides information about relationships among our inputs and outputs, we have not tested those relationships through the measures we identified in this report. Therefore, researchers could closely examine those relationships to collect evidence on the validity of putting together the inputs, outputs, and constructs we identified.

In addition, our measures indicated considerable interstate and intrastate variation in civic infrastructure. Research to explore the implications of this variation for civic literacy, identity, and engagement would help both to validate our framework and to consider the compounding influence of variation across various types of civic inputs and outputs. For example, in a state where available measures show demonstrably lower ratings of democratic governance, civic education, and civic spaces, those low ratings could drive lower civic outcomes. When such intrastate data exist, researchers should consider exploiting that variation to understand how civic infrastructures might vary not only across states but within them.

We also have little understanding about which of the measures we have identified are most critical for civic outcomes and thus would be important areas of focus for development and growth. However, much more research would be necessary to explore that variation and its implications.

Implications for policy and practice. Our research also has several implications for policy and practice. *First, our research points to the need for new, comprehensive measures of civic infrastructure across the United States in many areas of civic infrastructure where—for example—we have international measures but not state-by-state ones or where we lack subgroup data, among other gaps.* Without these data, we cannot say anything conclusive about the extent of civic infrastructure across the United States and state-by-state variation. That said, data necessary to capture civic infrastructure requires considerable action and funding from policymakers and other organizations with the capacity to develop critical measures. Some examples of the types of actions that could yield more-useful measures of our civic infrastructure include the following:

- *Expand nationally representative datasets to provide more fine-grained data, in addition to national data.* For example, the NAEP assesses students' performance in civics in eighth grade every few years. If we had state-representative data from NAEP, we would have a more robust civic literacy measure to which we could compare state requirements and standards, as well as other civic infrastructure inputs. Furthermore, although many national surveys exist that examine civic identity, literacy, engagement, and other measures, those surveys typically do not gather state-level data. With more funding, they could do so and thus provide much more information on areas where civic infrastructure may be particularly low or high and, thus, potentially require more resources and interventions.
- *Increase accessibility and standardization of data.* Although voter turnout and registration data are available on a state-by-state basis, it is much harder to access for counties or parishes within states. In addition, states sometimes collect such data in different forms and provide information on platforms with limited usability. If the federal government required states to report certain metrics in a standardized fashion—and gave them necessary funding to do so—it would likely be easier to make comparisons within and across states. Likewise, if states collaborated, they could work together to identify similar measures to collect and share. The Electronic Registration Information Center (ERIC) is an example of a collaboration among states that work together to improve the accuracy of U.S. voter registration and voting data (Electronic Registration Information Center, undated).
- *Prioritize U.S. participation in international data collection activities.* Although some international data include information from the United States, such as Freedom House ratings, other international data would require U.S. cooperation, such as the International Civic and Citizenship Education Study, which the United States has not participated in since 1999. By participating in these international data collections, the United States can better gauge where it stands in comparison with other nations and whether civic infrastructure trends in

the United States mirror or conflict with international trends, which might suggest greater areas of concern for further civic infrastructure development.

Second, although this research is preliminary, it has a few potential implications for steps we could explore to strengthen our civic infrastructure. One is that *the proliferation of state legislation both expanding and restricting political and social rights will likely lead to considerable inequities across states and communities in regard to rights and access to civic education, civic spaces, and civic engagement.* The parallel findings from Freedom House and others that U.S. democracy is declining in some ways suggests that we need to engage in urgent and earnest investigation of what aspects of civic infrastructure should be consistent and help us decrease differences in such outputs as civic literacy, identity, and engagement. Such an investigation could be undertaken at the federal level but also potentially through state networks that are committed to strengthen particular aspects of civic infrastructure, such as civic education or civic spaces. The Council of Chief State School Officers, for example, gathers together state education officials on a regular basis to support their reform efforts and could be a focal organization supporting K–12 civic education in particular. Similar organizations could support state networks in other areas, such as increasing civic spaces and engagement.

Relatedly, our research points to the growing diversity in some government positions alongside data suggesting that government officials in the United States are considerably older than in other nations. *These data suggest the need for education and engagement initiatives that inspire youth and younger generations to get involved in politics and in efforts that help them make a difference in their community.* By driving more interest in politics and government, such efforts might lead to even greater diversity in those roles and help democratic governance evolve demographically at the same rate as the population.

As we noted in the introduction, this report is intended to provide a starting point for defining and measuring civic infrastructure. With more collaboration and attention to the factors that support civic outcomes, we can work to build the civic infrastructure that everyone in the United States deserves.

Civic Infrastructure Measure Data Sources

This table provides additional information about the data sources included in Tables 2.1 through 2.6 that are example measures for the civic infrastructure inputs and outputs in our framework. For each data source, we include a little additional detail on what is measured, the organization that provides and owns the data, and how the data can be accessed.

TABLE A.1

List of Data Sources for Each Measure and How to Access Them

Civic Infrastructure Input or Output	Measure	Organization That Owns the Data	How to Access (including information on data format)
Democratic governance	Degree of democratic governance, as reflected by Global Freedom rating capturing a variety of information about political rights and civil liberties	Freedom House	Data available in the interactive data tool (Freedom House, undated-a) and in a series of web summary tables (Freedom House, undated-b). Separate webpages for each country contain more-detailed information (Freedom House, undated-e). Data updated annually.
	A large variety of election law and procedural processes, including absentee voting, alternative voting methods, voter ID and registration, election security, and more	NCSL	Data available in multiple formats (NCSL, 2022b) including a database (NCSL, 2022c), annual summary reports (NCSL, 2022a), and shorter, topically focused blog posts. Data updated annually.
	Statewide laws and policies that affect LBGTQ+ people and their families	HRC&EF	Data available in state scorecards (HRC&EF, undated-b), summary reports (HRC&EF, undated-a), and summary maps (HRC&EF, 2022). Data updated annually.
	Citizen access to justice	OECD	Country-level data available in Figures 14.10 and 14.11 in OECD's *Government at a Glance 2021* summary report (OECD, 2021b). Summary tables can be downloaded in an Excel format using the link on the same page in the PDF.

Table A.1—Continued

Civic Infrastructure Input or Output	Measure	Organization That Owns the Data	How to Access (including information on data format)
Democratic governance	Perceptions of public sector corruption	Transparency International	Country-level data available over time in an interactive data tool (Transparency International, undated). A dataset can be downloaded along with a summary report, maps, and infographics.
	Demographic composition in government and elected positions	OECD	Country-level data available in Chapter 3 in the OECD's *Government at a Glance 2021* summary report (OECD, 2021b). Summary tables can be downloaded in an Excel format using the links in the PDF.
	Demographic composition of state legislatures	NCSL	State-level data available in an interactive data tool (NCSL, 2020). Data available for 2015 and 2020.
	Demographic composition of federal legislature	Pew Research Center	Data available over time and by subgroup (for example, race/ethnicity, gender, age, immigrant status, and military background) in several summary figures (Schaeffer 2021a; Schaeffer, 2021b).
	State provisions related to disability protections	Bloomberg Law	Data are available in an interactive map as well as summary report that outlines key laws in each state (Bloomberg Law, 2021).

Table A.1—Continued

Civic Infrastructure Input or Output	Measure	Organization That Owns the Data	How to Access (including information on data format)
Civic education	K–12 course requirements for civics and civics topics covered	Brookings Institution	State-level data available in Chapter 2 of a recent report (Hansen et al., 2018).
	Ratings for K–12 state academic standards in civics and U.S. history	Fordham Institute	State-level data available in a recent report (Stern et al., 2021) and summary map.
	K–12 media literacy standards	Media Literacy Now	State-level information (for 14 states only) available in a recent report (Media Literacy Now, 2020).
	Civics education requirements (for example, courses, curriculum, community service, exams)	Center for American Progress	State-level data available in Figure 1 of a recent report (Shapiro and Brown, 2018).
	Legislative efforts to restrict and expand education on racism, bias, the contributions of specific racial or ethnic groups to U.S. history	Education Week	State-level data available in an interactive data tool (Schwartz, 2022) and database.
		Chalkbeat	State-level data available in an interactive data tool (Stout and Wilburn, 2022). Data can also be downloaded on same webpage.
	K–12 students' participation in various civic learning opportunities, according to teacher self-report	RAND Corporation	Summary findings—primarily at the national level and by subgroup—available in a report (Hamilton, Kaufman, and Hu, 2020).

Table A.1—Continued

Civic Infrastructure Input or Output	Measure	Organization That Owns the Data	How to Access (including information on data format)
Civic spaces	Internet access	U.S. Census Bureau	Data by state, county, and subgroup available in a recent report (Martin, 2021) using data from the 2018 American Community Survey. More-recent and comprehensive data in the data.census.gov data tool (U.S. Census, undated).
		Pew Research Center	Data available by subgroup and over time in a series of summary figures (Pew Research Center, 2021b).
		OECD	Country-level data available in Figure 2.1 of a recent report (OECD, 2021a). Summary tables can be downloaded in an Excel format using the links in the PDF. Data collection conducted every three years.
		Federal Communications Commission	Data are available in an interactive map (Federal Communications Commission, undated). Raw data can also be downloaded on the same page.
	Social media use among tweens and teens	Common Sense Media	Data available by subgroup and over time on pages 33 and 34 of a recent report (Rideout et al., 2022).

Table A.1—Continued

Civic Infrastructure Input or Output	Measure	Organization That Owns the Data	How to Access (including information on data format)
Civic spaces	Access to parks	Trust for Public Land	City-level data (for only the 100 largest cities) available over time in an interactive data tool (Trust for Public Land, undated).
	Access to public libraries and their use	Institute of Museum and Library Services	Data files can be downloaded from Institute of Museum and Library Services, undated
	Newspaper deserts	University of North Carolina Hussman School of Journalism and Media	State- and county-level data are available in an interactive data tool (Tableau Public, 2020). Key findings also summarized in a report (University of North Carolina Hussman School of Journalism and Media, undated).
	Access to and participation in civic spaces	Reimagining the Civic Commons	Baseline (Reimagining the Civic Commons, undated-b) and interim (Reimagining the Civic Commons, undated-c) city-level data available for Akron, Ohio; Chicago, Illinois; Detroit, Michigan; and Memphis, Tennessee, via summary reports.
	Internet freedom	Freedom House	Data available in an interactive data tool (Freedom House, undated-c). Data can also be downloaded in Excel files (Freedom House, undated-d) and are summarized in annual reports available on the same page.

Table A.1—Continued

Civic Infrastructure Input or Output	Measure	Organization That Owns the Data	How to Access (including information on data format)
Civic literacy	Student proficiency in grades 4, 8, and 12 on a national civics assessment	NCES	Data from NAEP available in summary reports (NAEP, 2021) and in the NAEP Data Explorer (Nation's Report Card, undated-b), an interactive data tool. Application to and approval by U.S. Department of Education required to access raw data files.
	U.S adults' knowledge of the Constitution and how government works	Annenberg Public Policy Center	Data available as summarized statistics in annual reports (Annenberg Public Policy Center, undated).
	Proficiency in distinguishing facts from opinions among 15-year-olds	OECD	Country-level data available in Figures 2.4 and 2.5 of a recent report (OECD, 2021a). Summary tables can be downloaded in an Excel format using the links in the PDF. Data collection conducted every three years (although this question may not be repeated in the future).
	Proficiency in literacy and numeracy skills among all adults ages 16–74	NCES & OECD	Data available at state- and county-levels in an interactive data tool (Programme for the International Assessment of Adult Competencies [PIAAC], undated). Raw data can be downloaded from this data tool. Key data by subgroup for the United States available in a recent summary report (NCES, undated-a). To compare the United States with other countries, use the PIAAC International Data Explorer (NCES, undated-b), an interactive data tool.

Table A.1—Continued

Civic Infrastructure Input or Output	Measure	Organization That Owns the Data	How to Access (including information on data format)
Civic identity	Political party affiliation	Gallup	Data available over time in web summary tables (Gallup, undated-a).
		Pew Research Center	Data available by subgroup and over time in a series of summary figures (Pew Research Center, 2020).
		Pew Research Center	State-level data available in a web summary table and figure (Pew Research Center, undated).
	Political ideology (liberal-conservative) self-identification	ANES	Trend data available in a web summary table and figure (ANES, undated-f). Raw data files can also be downloaded to produce subgroup estimates.
	Public opinion monitoring pride in being an American	Gallup	Data available by subgroup and over time in a brief series of web tables and figures (Jones, 2021).

Table A.1—Continued

Civic Infrastructure Input or Output	Measure	Organization That Owns the Data	How to Access (including information on data format)
Civic identity	Trust and confidence in government	Gallup	Data available over time in web summary tables (Gallup, undated-b).
		Pew Research Center	Data available by subgroup and over time in a brief series of web tables and figures (Pew Research Center, 2022).
		OECD	Country-level data available over time in an interactive data tool (OECD, undated-b). Data can also be downloaded.
		Gallup	State-level data available in a brief series of web tables and figures (Jones, 2014).
	Extent to which people perceive voting as a civic duty versus a choice	ANES	Trend data available in the continuity guide (ANES, undated-a) if searched by survey item. Raw data files can also be downloaded to produce subgroup estimates.
	Political efficacy index	ANES	Trend data available in a web summary table and figure (ANES, undated-d). Raw data files can also be downloaded to produce subgroup estimates.

Table A.1—Continued

Civic Infrastructure Input or Output	Measure	Organization That Owns the Data	How to Access (including information on data format)
Civic engagement	Proportion of individuals that is registered to vote among the eligible voting population	U.S. Census Bureau	Trend data (U.S. Census Bureau, 2021b); subgroup and state-level data available in a series of downloadable Excel tables (U.S. Census Bureau, 2021a).
	Voter turnout for elections	United States Election Project	Multiple state- and local-level datasets available to download, including data over time (United States Election Project, undated).
		U.S. Census Bureau	Trend data (U.S. Census Bureau, 2021b); subgroup and state-level data available in a series of downloadable Excel tables (U.S. Census Bureau, 2021a).
		OECD	Country-level data available in short country-specific reports (OECD Better Life index, undated). Raw country-level data can be downloaded from OECD.Stat, an interactive data tool.
	Percentage of individuals who financially supported a political campaign	ANES	Trend data available in a web summary table and figure (ANES, undated-e). Raw data files can also be downloaded to produce subgroup estimates.

Table A.1—Continued

Civic Infrastructure Input or Output	Measure	Organization That Owns the Data	How to Access (including information on data format)
Civic engagement	Percentage of individuals who indicated that they attended a political event	ANES	Trend data available in a web summary table and figure (ANES, undated-c). Raw data files can also be downloaded to produce subgroup estimates.
	Percentage of individuals who indicated that they participated in a protest, march, or demonstration	ANES	Trend data available in the continuity guide (ANES, undated-a) if searched by survey item. Raw data files can also be downloaded to produce subgroup estimates.
	Political demonstrations and political violence	Armed Conflict Location & Event Data Project	Data available in a series of web figures (Armed Conflict Location & Event Data Project, 2020) and a more comprehensive report (Armed Conflict Location & Event Data Project, 2021).
		Bridging Divides Initiative, Princeton University	Various data available in a map, downloadable database, and series of reports (Bridging Divides Initiative at Princeton, undated).

Table A.1—Continued

Civic Infrastructure Input or Output	Measure	Organization That Owns the Data	How to Access (including information on data format)
Civic engagement	Percentage of individuals who indicated that they contacted a public official at any level of government	U.S. Census Bureau	Data, including estimates over time, by state and by subgroup available on data.census.gov, an interactive data tool (U.S. Census Bureau, undated). To our knowledge, there are no ready-made published estimates of these data.
	Percentage of individuals who indicated that they volunteered at an organization or association	U.S. Census Bureau	Data, including estimates over time, by state and by subgroup available on data.census.gov, an interactive data tool (U.S. Census Bureau, undated). To our knowledge, there are no ready-made published estimates of these data.
	Frequency of discussing political, societal, or local issues with family, friends, and neighbors	U.S. Census Bureau	Data, including estimates over time, by state and by subgroup available on data.census.gov, an interactive data tool (U.S. Census Bureau, undated). To our knowledge, there are no ready-made published estimates of these data.
	Frequency of posting views about political, societal, or local issues on social media	U.S. Census Bureau	Data, including estimates over time, by state and by subgroup available on data.census.gov, an interactive data tool (U.S. Census Bureau, undated). To our knowledge, there are no ready-made published estimates of these data.

Abbreviations

ANES	American National Election Studies
COVID-19	coronavirus disease 2019
HRC&EF	Human Rights Campaign Foundation and Equality Federation Institute
K–12	kindergarten through 12th grade
NAEP	National Assessment of Educational Progress
NCOC	National Conference on Citizenship
NCSL	National Conference of State Legislatures
OECD	Organisation for Economic Co-Operation and Development

References

Abernathy, Penelope Muse, *News Deserts and Ghost Newspapers: Will Local News Survive?* University of North Carolina Hussman School of Journalism and Media, 2020.

Adler, Richard P., and Judy Goggin, "What Do We Mean By 'Civic Engagement'?" *Journal of Transformative Education,* Vol. 3, No. 3, 2005, pp. 236–253.

Allen, B. J., Jr., "Revitalizing Citizenship Education," *Social Studies*, Vol. 70, No. 6, 1979, pp. 246–250.

American National Election Studies, "ANES Continuity Guide," undated-a. As of June 1, 2022:
https://electionstudies.org/resources/anes-continuity-guide/

―――, "ANES Question Search," webpage, undated-b. As of June 1, 2022:
https://electionstudies.org/resources/anes-question-search/

―――, "Attended Political Meeting 1952–2020," summary tables, undated-c. As of August 12, 2022:
https://electionstudies.org/resources/anes-guide/top-tables/?id=72

―――, "External Political Efficacy Index 1952-2020," summary tables, undated-d. As of August 12, 2022:
https://electionstudies.org/resources/anes-guide/top-tables/?id=117

―――, "Gave Money to Help a Campaign 1952–2020," summary tables, undated-e. As of August 12, 2022:
https://electionstudies.org/resources/anes-guide/top-tables/?id=75

―――, "Liberal-Conservative Self-Identification 1972–2020," web summary table, undated-f. As of August 12, 2022:
https://electionstudies.org/resources/anes-guide/top-tables/?id=29

ANES—*See* American National Election Studies.

Annenberg Public Policy Center, "Annenberg Civics Knowledge Survey," webpage, undated. As of May 5, 2022:
https://www.annenbergpublicpolicycenter.org/political-communication/civics-knowledge-survey/

―――, "Americans' Civics Knowledge Increases During a Stress-Filled Year," webpage, September 14, 2021. As of June 2, 2022:
https://www.annenbergpublicpolicycenter.org/2021-annenberg-constitution-day-civics-survey/

Armed Conflict Location & Event Data Project, "Demonstrations and Political Violence in America: New Data for Summer 2020," web figures, September 3, 2020. As of June 2, 2022:
https://acleddata.com/2020/09/03/demonstrations-political-violence-in-america-new-data-for-summer-2020/

———, *A Year of Racial Justice Protests: Key Trends in Demonstrations Supporting the BLM Movement*, May 2021.

Arnberger, Arne, and Renate Eder, "The Influence of Green Space on Community Attachment of Urban and Suburban Residents," *Urban Forestry & Urban Greening*, Vol. 11, No. 1, 2012, pp. 41–49.

Ashley, Seth, Adam Maksl, and Stephanie Craft, "News Media Literacy and Political Engagement: What's the Connection?" *Journal of Media Literacy Education*, Vol. 9, No. 1, 2017, pp. 79–98.

Atwell, Matthew, Bennett Stillerman, and John M. Bridgeland, *Civic Health Index 2021: Citizenship Curing Crisis*, National Conference on Citizenship, 2021.

Bakker, Tom P., and Claes H. de Vreese, "Good News for the Future? Young People, Internet Use, and Political Participation," *Communication Research*, Vol. 38, No. 4, 2011, pp. 451–470.

Baskin-Sommers, Arielle, Cortney Simmons, May Conley, and B. J. Casey, "Adolescent Civic Engagement: Lessons from Black Lives Matter," *PNAS*, Vol. 118, No. 41, 2021.

Bauhr, Monika, Marcia Grimes, and Niklas Harring, *Seeing the State: The Implications of Transparency for Societal Accountability*, University of Gothenburg, Quality of Government Institute, QoG Working Paper Series 2010:15, 2010.

Blair, Jill, and Malka Kopell, *21st Century Civic Infrastructure: Under Construction*, Aspen Institute Forum for Community Solutions, 2015.

Bloomberg Law, "Disability Discrimination Laws by State," December 20, 2021.

Bogart, William T., *Civic Infrastructure and the Financing of Community Development*, York College of Pennsylvania, Brookings Institution Center on Urban and Metropolitan Policy, 2003.

Boggs, Carl, "Social Capital and Political Fantasy: Robert Putnam's 'Bowling Alone,'" *Theory and Society*, Vol. 30, No. 2, 2001, pp. 281–297.

Brady, Henry E., "Political Participation," in John P. Robinson, Phillip R. Shaver, and Lawrence S. Wrightsman, eds., *Measures of Political Attitudes*, Academic Press, 1999.

Brandtzæg, Petter Bae, Asbjørn Følstad, and Henry Mainsah, *Designing for Youth Civic Engagement in Social Media*, International Association for Development of the Information Society, 2012.

Brenan, Megan, "Americans' Confidence in Major U.S. Institutions Dips," Pew Research Center, July 14, 2021. As of June 10, 2022:
https://news.gallup.com/poll/352316/
americans-confidence-major-institutions-dips.aspx

Bridging Divides Initiative, Princeton University, homepage, undated. As of October 12, 2022:
https://bridgingdivides.princeton.edu/

Burkhart, Annalise, "Corruption in the U.S.: Is Change Coming?" Transparency International blog post, February 17, 2021. As of October 12, 2022:
https://www.transparency.org/en/blog/cpi-2020-corruption-united-states

Chae, Younggil, Sookjung Lee, and Yeolib Kim, "Meta-Analysis of the Relationship Between Internet Use and Political Participation: Examining Main and Moderating Effects," *Asian Journal of Communication,* Vol. 29, No. 1, 2019, pp. 35–54.

Commission on the Practice of Democratic Citizenship, *Our Common Purpose: Reinventing American Democracy for the 21st Century*, American Academy of Arts and Sciences, 2020.

Council of Chief State School Officers, "The Marginalization of Social Studies," fact sheet, 2018.

Dalton, Russell J., David M. Farrell, and Ian McAllister, *Political Parties and Democratic Linkage: How Parties Organize Democracy*, Oxford University Press, 2011.

Daniels, Jessie, *Cyber Racism: White Supremacy Online and the New Attack on Civil Rights*, Rowman & Littlefield, 2009.

Diller, E. C., *Citizens in Service: The Challenge of Delivering Civic Engagement Training to National Service Programs*, Corporation for National and Community Service, 2001.

Diliberti, Melissa Kay, and Heather L. Schwartz, *Districts Continue to Struggle with Staffing, Political Polarization, and Unfinished Instruction: Selected Findings from the Fifth American School District Panel Survey*, RAND Corporation, RR-A956-13, 2022. As of September 28, 2022:
https://www.rand.org/pubs/research_reports/RRA956-13.html

Doherty, David, and Jennifer Wolak, "When Do the Ends Justify the Means? Evaluating Procedural Fairness," *Political Behavior,* Vol. 34, No. 2, June 2012, pp. 301–323.

Downs-Karkos, Susan, and Rachel Peric, *Building Cohesive Communities in an Era of Migration and Change*, Welcoming America, 2019. https://welcomingamerica.org/wp-content/uploads/2021/04/Building-Cohesive-Communities_FINAL.pdf

Durlauf, Steven N., "Bowling Alone: A Review Essay," *Journal of Economic Behavior & Organization*, Vol. 47, No. 3, 2002, pp. 259–273.

Ebert, Kim, and Dina G. Okamoto, "Social Citizenship, Integration and Collective Action: Immigrant Civic Engagement in the United States," *Social Forces*, Vol. 91, No. 4, 2013, pp. 1267–1292.

Edrington, Candice L., and Nicole Lee, "Tweeting a Social Movement: Black Lives Matter and Its Use of Twitter to Share Information, Build Community, and Promote Action," *Journal of Public Interest Communications*, Vol. 2, No. 2, 2018, pp. 289–306.

Ekman, Joakim, and Erik Amnå, "Political Participation and Civic Engagement: Towards a New Typology," *Human Affairs*, Vol. 22, No. 3, 2012, pp. 283–300.

Electronic Registration Information Center, homepage, undated. As of June 2, 2022: https://ericstates.org/

Ellison, Nicole B., Charles Steinfield, and Cliff Lampe, "The Benefits of Facebook 'Friends': Social Capital and College Students' Use of Online Social Network Sites," *Journal of Computer-Mediated Communication*, Vol. 12, No. 4, 2007, pp. 1143–1168.

Evans, Sara M., and Harry C. Boyte, *Free Spaces: The Sources of Democratic Change in America*, University of Chicago Press, 1992.

FairVote, "Voter Turnout," webpage, undated. As of June 1, 2022: https://www.fairvote.org/voter_turnout#voter_turnout_101

Federal Communications Commission, "Fixed Broadband Deployment," webpage, undated. As of June 2, 2022: https://broadband477map.fcc.gov/#/

Feeney, Mary, Eric Welch, and Meg Haller, *Transparency, Civic Engagement, and Technology Use in Local Government Agencies: Findings from a National Survey*, University of Illinois at Chicago, Institute for Policy and Civic Engagement, 2011.

Fishkin, James S., and Robert C. Luskin, "Bringing Deliberation to the Democratic Dialogue," in Maxwell McCombs and Amy Reynolds, eds., *The Poll with A Human Face: The National Issues Convention Experiment in Political Communication*, Routledge, 1999.

Foad, Colin M. G., Lorraine Whitmarsh, Paul H. P. Hanel, and Geoffrey Haddock, "The Limitations of Polling Data in Understanding Public Support for COVID-19 Lockdown Policies," *Royal Society Open Science*, Vol. 8, No. 7, July 7, 2021.

Franklin, Mark N., "Electoral Engineering and Cross-National Turnout Differences: What Role for Compulsory Voting?" *British Journal of Political Science*, Vol. 29, No. 1, 1999.

Freedom House, "Change in Democracy Status," data tool, undated-a. As of October 13, 2022:
https://freedomhouse.org/
explore-the-map?type=nit&year=2022&mapview=trend

———, Countries and Territories, summary tables, undated-b. As of October 13, 2022:
https://freedomhouse.org/countries/freedom-world/scores

———, "Internet Freedom Status," undated-c. As of June 10, 2022:
https://freedomhouse.org/explore-the-map?type=fotn&year=2021

———, "Freedom on the Net," webpage, undated-d. As of June 1, 2022:
https://freedomhouse.org/report/freedom-net

———, "Freedom in the World 2022: United States," webpage, undated-e. As of June 1, 2022:
https://freedomhouse.org/country/united-states/freedom-world/2022

Gallup, "Party Affiliation," webpage, undated-a. As of June 2, 2022:
https://news.gallup.com/poll/15370/party-affiliation.aspx

———, "Trust in Government," webpage, undated-b. As of June 2, 2022:
https://news.gallup.com/poll/5392/trust-government.aspx

Gastil, John, and Michael Xenos, "Of Attitudes and Engagement: Clarifying the Reciprocal Relationship Between Civic Attitudes and Political Participation," *Journal of Communication*, Vol. 60, No. 2, 2010, pp. 318–343.

Gates, C. T., "The National Civic Index: A New Approach to Community Problem Solving," *National Civic Review*, Vol. 76, No. 6, 1987, pp. 472–479.

Gordon, Eric, and Paul Mihailidis, *Civic Media: Technology, Design, Practice*, Massachusetts Institute of Technology Press, 2016.

Gros, Maya, and Norman Eisen, "Digitizing Civic Spaces amid the COVID-19 Pandemic and Beyond," *Up Front*, blog post, Brookings Institution, 2021. As of June 1, 2022:
https://www.brookings.edu/blog/up-front/2021/03/09/
digitizing-civic-spaces-amid-the-covid-19-pandemic-and-beyond/

Gould, Jonathan, ed., *Guardian of Democracy: The Civic Mission of Schools*, Campaign for the Civic Mission of Schools, Leonore Annenberg Institute for Civics of the Annenberg Public Policy Center at the University of Pennsylvania, the National Conference on Citizenship, the Center for Information and Research on Civic Learning and Engagement at Tufts University, and the American Bar Association Division for Public Education, 2011.

Hamilton, Laura S., Julia H. Kaufman, and Lynn Hu, *Preparing Children and Youth for Civic Life in the Era of Truth Decay: Insights from the American Teacher Panel*, RAND Corporation, RR-A112-6, 2020. As of September 28, 2022:
https://www.rand.org/pubs/research_reports/RRA112-6.html

Hansen, Michael, Elizabeth Mann-Levesque, Jon Valant, and Diana Quintero, *The 2018 Brown Center Report on American Education*, Brookings Institution, 2018.

Hart, Daniel, Thomas M. Donnelly, James Youniss, and Robert Atkins, "High School Community Service as a Predictor of Adult Voting and Volunteering," *American Educational Research Journal*, Vol. 44, No. 1, 2007, pp. 197–219.

Hart, Daniel, Cameron Richardson, and Britt Wilkenfeld, "Civic Identity," in Seth J. Schwartz, Koen Luyckx, and Vivian L. Vignoles, eds., *Handbook of Identity Theory and Research*, Springer, 2011.

Heafner, Tina L., and Paul G. Fitchett, "Tipping the Scales: National Trends of Declining Social Studies Instructional Time in Elementary Schools," *Journal of Social Studies Research*, Vol. 36, No. 2, 2012.

Herczog, Michelle M., "The Links Between the C3 Framework and the NCSS National Curriculum Standards for Social Studies," *Social Education*, Vol. 77, No. 6, 2013, pp. 331–333.

HRC&EF—*See* Human Rights Campaign Foundation and Equality Federation Institute.

Huguet, Alice, Jennifer Kavanagh, Garrett Baker, and Marjory S. Blumenthal, *Exploring Media Literacy Education as a Tool for Mitigating Truth Decay*, RAND Corporation, RR-3050-RC, 2019. As of September 28, 2022:
https://www.rand.org/pubs/research_reports/RR3050.html

Human Rights Campaign Foundation and Equality Federation Institute, "Equality from State to State & State Equality Index Archives," webpage, undated-a. As of June 10, 2022:
https://www.hrc.org/resources/equality-from-state-to-state

———, "State Scorecards" webpage, undated-b. As of June 10, 2022:
https://www.hrc.org/resources/state-scorecards

———, "2021 State Equality Index," webpage, January 19, 2022. As of June 1, 2022:
https://www.hrc.org/resources/state-equality-index

Hylton, Mary E., "The Role of Civic Literacy and Social Empathy on Rates of Civic Engagement Among University Students," *Journal of Higher Education Outreach and Engagement*, Vol. 22, No. 1, 2018, p. 87.

Illinois Civic Hub, "Elements of Democracy Schools," webpage, undated. As of June 1, 2022:
https://www.illinoiscivics.org/democracy-schools/
elements-of-democracy-schools/

Institute of Museum and Library Services, "Public Libraries Survey," webpage, undated. As of June 2, 2022:
https://www.imls.gov/research-evaluation/data-collection/
public-libraries-survey

International Association for the Evaluation of Educational Achievement, "International Civic and Citizenship Education Study," webpage, undated. As of October 12, 2022:
https://www.iea.nl/studies/iea/iccs

Jackman, Robert W., "Political Institutions and Voter Turnout in the Industrial Democracies," *American Political Science Review*, Vol. 81, No. 2, 1987, pp. 405–423.

John, Peter, and Alistair Cole, "Urban Regimes and Local Governance in Britain and France: Policy Adaption and Coordination in Leeds and Lille," *Urban Affairs Review*, Vol. 33, No. 3, 1998, pp. 382–404.

Jones, Dustin, and Jonathan Franklin, "Not Just Florida. More Than a Dozen States Propose So-Called 'Don't Say Gay' Bills," NPR, April 10, 2022. As of June 1, 2022:
https://www.npr.org/2022/04/10/1091543359/
15-states-dont-say-gay-anti-transgender-bills

Jones, Jeffrey M., "Illinois Residents Least Trusting of Their State Government," Gallup, April 4, 2014. As of June 1, 2022:
https://news.gallup.com/poll/168251/
illinois-residents-least-trusting-state-government.aspx#1

Jones, Jeffrey M., "American Pride Ticks Up From Last Year's Record Low," Gallup, July 1, 2021. As of June 1, 2022:
https://news.gallup.com/poll/351791/
american-pride-ticks-last-year-record-low.aspx

Kahne, Joseph E., and Susan E. Sporte, "Developing Citizens: The Impact of Civic Learning Opportunities on Students' Commitment to Civic Participation," *American Educational Research Journal*, Vol. 45, No. 3, 2008, pp. 738–766.

Kavanagh, Jennifer, Katherine Grace Carman, Maria DeYoreo, Nathan Chandler, and Lynn E. Davis, *The Drivers of Institutional Trust and Distrust: Exploring Components of Trustworthiness*, RAND Corporation, RR-A112-7, 2020. As of September 27, 2022:
https://www.rand.org/pubs/research_reports/RRA112-7.html

Kavanagh, Jennifer, and Michael D. Rich, *Truth Decay: An Initial Exploration of the Diminishing Role of Facts and Analysis in American Public Life*, RAND Corporation, RR-2314-RC, 2018. As of September 27, 2022:
https://www.rand.org/pubs/research_reports/RR2314.html

Keeter, Scott, Cliff Zukin, Molly Andolina, and Krista Jenkins, *The Civic and Political Health of the Nation: A Generational Portrait*, Center for Information and Research on Civic Learning and Engagement (CIRCLE), 2002.

Kenski, Kate, and Natalie Jomini Stroud, "Connections Between Internet Use and Political Efficacy, Knowledge, and Participation," *Journal of Broadcasting & Electronic Media*, Vol. 50, No. 2, 2006, pp. 173–192.

Knefelkamp, L. Lee, "Civic Identity: Locating Self in Community," *Diversity & Democracy*, Vol. 11, No. 2, 2008.

Korn, Matthias, and Amy Voida, "Creating Friction: Infrastructuring Civic Engagement in Everyday Life," paper presented at the Fifth Decennial Aarhus Conference on Critical Alternatives, 2015.

Kukovetz, Brigitte, and Annette Sprung, "Transformative Civic Learning Within Volunteering in Refugee Relief," in Chad Hoggan and Tetyana Hoggan-Kloubert, eds., *Adult Learning in a Migration Society*, Routledge, 2021.

Kuo, Frances E., William C. Sullivan, Rebekah Levine Coley, and Liesette Brunson, "Fertile Ground for Community: Inner-City Neighborhood Common Spaces," *American Journal of Community Psychology*, Vol. 26, No. 6, 1998, pp. 823–851.

Lauglo, Jon, "Political Socialization in the Family and Young People's Educational Achievement and Ambition," *British Journal of Sociology of Education*, Vol. 32, No. 1, 2011, pp. 53–74.

Lawless, Jennifer L., "Politics of Presence? Congresswomen and Symbolic Representation," *Political Research Quarterly*, Vol. 57, No. 1, 2004, pp. 81–99.

Levine, Peter, "Collective Action, Civic Engagement, and the Knowledge Commons," in Charlotte Hess and Elinor Ostrom, eds., *Understanding Knowledge as a Commons: From Theory to Practice*, Massachusetts Institute of Technology Press, 2006.

Levine, Peter, and Kei Kawashima-Ginsberg, *The Republic Is (Still) at Risk—and Civics Is Part of the Solution*, Jonathan M. Tisch College of Civic Life, Tufts University, 2017.

Lewicka, Maria, "Place Attachment: How Far Have We Come in the Last 40 Years?" *Journal of Environmental Psychology*, Vol. 31, No. 3, 2011, pp. 207–230.

Liu, Baodong, Sharon D. Wright Austin, and Byron D'Andrá Orey, "Church Attendance, Social Capital, and Black Voting Participation," *Social Science Quarterly*, Vol. 90, No. 3, 2009, pp. 576–592.

Luskin, Robert C., James S. Fishkin, and Roger Jowell, "Considered Opinions: Deliberative Polling in Britain," *British Journal of Political Science*, Vol. 32, No. 3, 2002, pp. 455–487.

Mabry, J. Beth, "Pedagogical Variations in Service-Learning and Student Outcomes: How Time, Contact, and Reflection Matter," *Michigan Journal of Community Service Learning*, Vol. 5, No. 1, 1998, pp. 32–47.

Manago, Adriana, Nicholas Santer, Logan L. Barsigian, and Abigail Walsh, "Social Media as Tools for Cultural Change in the Transition to Adulthood," in Kate C. McLean, ed., *Cultural Methods in Psychology: Describing and Transforming Cultures*, Oxford University Press, 2021, pp. 146–173.

Martens, Hans, and Renee Hobbs, "How Media Literacy Supports Civic Engagement in a Digital Age," *Atlantic Journal of Communication*, Vol. 23, No. 2, 2015, pp. 120–137.

Martin, Michael, *Computer and Internet Use in the United States: 2018*, Washington, D.C.: Census Bureau, 2021.

Mathews, Nick, "Life in a News Desert: The Perceived Impact of a Newspaper Closure on Community Members," *Journalism*, Vol. 23, No. 6, 2022, pp. 1250–1265.

McGrew, Sarah, Joel Breakstone, Teresa Ortega, Mark Smith, and Sam Wineburg, "Can Students Evaluate Online Sources? Learning from Assessments of Civic Online Reasoning," *Theory & Research in Social Education,* Vol. 46, No. 2, 2018, pp. 165–193.

McShane, Ian, Chris Wilson, and Denise Meredyth, "Broadband as Civic Infrastructure: The Australian Case," *Media International Australia*, Vol. 151, No. 1, 2014, pp. 127–136.

Media Literacy Now, "Putting Media Literacy on the Public Policy Agenda," webpage, undated. As of June 1, 2022:
https://medialiteracynow.org/your-state-legislation-2/

———, *U.S. Media Literacy Policy Report 2020*, January 2020.

Mellor, Suzanne, "Insights from Formal Testing of Civics and Citizenship Learning in Australia," *Citizenship Teaching and Learning*, Vol. 6, No. 1, 2010, pp. 25–42.

Miles, Matthew R., "Turnout as Consent: How Fair Governance Encourages Voter Participation," *Political Research Quarterly*, Vol. 68, No. 2, 2015, pp. 363–376.

Miller, Judith, "News Deserts: No News Is Bad News," Urban Policy 2018: Manhattan Institute, 2018.

Mitchell, Tania D., "Using a Critical Service-Learning Approach to Facilitate Civic Identity Development," *Theory into Practice*, Vol. 54, No. 1, 2015, pp. 20–28.

Montinola, Gabriella R., and Robert W. Jackman, "Sources of Corruption: A Cross-Country Study," *British Journal of Political Science*, Vol. 32, No. 1, 2002, pp. 147–170.

Moss, Robert, *Democracy: A Case Study*, Harvard University Press, 2017.

Moy, Patricia, and Dietram A. Scheufele, "Media Effects on Political and Social Trust," *Journalism & Mass Communication Quarterly*, Vol. 77, No. 4, 2000, pp. 744–759.

NAEP—*See* National Assessment of Educational Progress.

National Assessment of Educational Progress, "Civics," September 20, 2021. As of February 22, 2022:
https://nces.ed.gov/nationsreportcard/civics/

National Center for Education Statistics, "Highlights of PIAAC 2017 U.S. Results," webpage, undated-a. As of June 2, 2022:
https://nces.ed.gov/surveys/piaac/national_results.asp

———, "IDE," data tool, undated-b. As of June 2, 2022:
https://nces.ed.gov/surveys/international/ide/

National Civic League, *Civic Index*, 4th ed., 2019. As of October 24, 2022:
https://www.nationalcivicleague.org/resources/civicindex/

National Conference of State Legislatures, "State Legislator Demographics," December 1, 2020. As of June 1, 2022:
https://www.ncsl.org/research/about-state-legislatures/
state-legislator-demographics.aspx

———, "Redistricting Systems: A 50-State Overview," March 29, 2021. As of June 1, 2022:
https://www.ncsl.org/research/redistricting/
redistricting-systems-a-50-state-overview.aspx

———, "The Canvass: January 2022," webpage, January 5, 2022a. As of June 1, 2022:
https://www.ncsl.org/research/elections-and-campaigns/
the-canvass-january-2022.aspx

———, "NCSL Election Resources," webpage, January 5, 2022b. As of June 1, 2022:
https://www.ncsl.org/research/elections-and-campaigns/
election-laws-and-procedures-overview.aspx

———, "State Elections Legislation Database," database, May 31, 2022c. As of June 5, 2022:
https://www.ncsl.org/research/elections-and-campaigns/
elections-legislation-database.aspx

National Conference on Citizenship, "Civic Health Initiative," webpage, undated. As of June 12, 2022:
https://ncoc.org/Civic-Health-Initiative-2/

———, *America's Civic Health Index: Broken Engagement*, 2006.

National Council for the Social Studies, *College, Career & Civic Life (C3) Framework for Social Studies State Standards: Guidance for Enhancing the Rigor of K–12 Civics, Economics, Geography, and History*, Silver Spring, Md., 2013.

National Women's Law Center, "State by State," webpage, undated. As of June 1, 2022:
https://nwlc.org/state-by-state/

Nation's Report Card, "Civics: Achievement-Level Results," webpage, undated-a. As of June 2, 2022:
https://www.nationsreportcard.gov/civics/results/achievement/

———, "NAEP Data Explorer," data tool, undated-b. As of June 12, 2022:
https://www.nationsreportcard.gov/ndecore/landing

NCES—*See* National Center for Education Statistics.

NCOC—*See* National Conference on Citizenship.

NCSL—*See* National Conference of State Legislatures.

Newport, Frank, "COVID and Americans' Trust in Government," Gallup, February 11, 2022. As of June 2, 2022:
https://news.gallup.com/opinion/polling-matters/389723/
covid-americans-trust-government.aspx

Notley, Tanya, Simon Chambers, Sora Park, and Michael Dezuanni, *Adult Media Literacy in Australia: Attitudes, Experiences and Needs*, Western Sydney University, Queensland University of Technology, and University of Canberra, 2021.

OECD—*See* Organisation for Economic Co-Operation and Development.

OECD Better Life Index, "Civic Engagement," webpage, undated. As of June 1, 2022:
https://www.oecdbetterlifeindex.org/topics/civic-engagement

Ognyanova, Katherine, Nien-Tsu Nancy Chen, Sandra J. Ball-Rokeach, Zheng An, Minhee Son, Michael Parks, and Daniela Gerson, "Online Participation in a Community Context: Civic Engagement and Connections to Local Communication Resources," *International Journal of Communication,* Vol. 7, 2013.

Open Government Partnership, "Actions to Protect and Enhance Civic Spaces," 2021. As of October 12, 2022:
https://www.opengovpartnership.org/
actions-for-a-secure-and-open-civic-space/

Organisation for Economic Co-Operation and Development, "Trust in Government," data tool, undated. As of June 1, 2022:
https://data.oecd.org/gga/trust-in-government.htm

———, *21st-Century Readers: Developing Literacy Skills in a Digital World*, 2021a.

———, *Government at a Glance 2021*, 2021b.

Pace, Judith L., "The Complex and Unequal Impact of High Stakes Accountability on Untested Social Studies," *Theory & Research in Social Education,* Vol. 39, No. 1, 2011, pp. 32–60.

Parr, John, "Civic Infrastructure: A New Approach to Improving Community Life," *National Civic Review,* Vol. 82, No. 2, 1993, pp. 93–100.

Patrick, Stephen, and Shari Brady, "Building an Intentional and Inclusive Civic Infrastructure," *Stanford Social Innovation Review,* August 7, 2015.

Pelczar, Marisa, Lisa M. Frehill, Evan Nielsen, Ashley Kaiser, J. Hudson, and T. Wan, *Characteristics of Public Libraries in the United States: Results from the FY 2019 Public Libraries Survey*, Washington, D.C.: Institute of Museum and Library Services, 2021.

Petrovska, Inha R., "Measuring Civic Identity: Difficulties and Solution," *Sociologija,* Vol. 24, No. 4, 2019, pp. 187–192.

Pew Research Center, "Party Affiliation by State," summary table, undated. As of June 1, 2022:
https://www.pewresearch.org/religion/religious-landscape-study/compare/
party-affiliation/by/state/

———, "Democratic Edge in Party Identification Narrows Slightly," June 2, 2020. As of June 1, 2022:
https://www.pewresearch.org/politics/2020/06/02/
democratic-edge-in-party-identification-narrows-slightly/

———, "Internet/Broadband Fact Sheet," summary figures, April 7, 2021a. As of June 2, 2022:
https://www.pewresearch.org/internet/fact-sheet/
internet-broadband/?menuItem=e60540d5-6342-47eb-835d-21b1c0a5e37b

———, "Who Has Home Broadband?" web figure, April 7, 2021b. As of June 2, 2022:
https://www.pewresearch.org/internet/fact-sheet/internet-broadband/?menuItem=e60540d5-6342-47eb-835d-21b1c0a5e37b

———, "Public Trust in Government: 1958–2022," June 6, 2022. As of June 10, 2022:
https://www.pewresearch.org/politics/2022/06/06/public-trust-in-government-1958-2022/

PIAAC—*See* Programme for the International Assessment of Adult Competencies.

Pollard, Michael S., and Jennifer Kavanagh, *Profiles of News Consumption: Platform Choices, Perceptions of Reliability, and Partisanship*, RAND Corporation, RR-4212-RC, 2019. As of September 27, 2022:
https://www.rand.org/pubs/research_reports/RR4212.html

Price, Vincent, Joseph N. Cappella, and Lilach Nir, "Does Disagreement Contribute to More Deliberative Opinion?" *Political Communication,* Vol. 19, No. 1, 2002, pp. 95–112.

Programme for the International Assessment of Adult Competencies, "U.S. Skills Map: State and County Indicators of Adult Literacy and Numeracy," webpage, undated. As of June 2, 2022:
https://nces.ed.gov/surveys/piaac/skillsmap/

Project for Public Spaces, "About: Great Public Spaces Strengthen Communities," webpage, undated. As of June 1, 2022:
https://www.pps.org/about

Putnam, Robert D., *Bowling Alone: The Collapse and Revival of American Community*, Simon and Schuster, 2000.

Putnam, Robert D., Robert Leonardi, and Raffaella Y. Nanetti, *Making Democracy Work: Civic Traditions in Modern Italy*, Princeton University Press, 1994.

Reimagining the Civic Commons, homepage, undated-a. As of June 2, 2022:
https://civiccommons.us/

———, "Baseline Metrics Reports," webpage, undated-b. As of June 2, 2022:
https://civiccommons.us/2018/05/baseline-metrics-reports/

———, Interim Metrics Reports, webpage, undated-c. As of June 2, 2022:
https://civiccommons.us/2019/04/interim-metrics-reports/

———, *Measuring the Civic Commons*, 2018.

Repucci, Sarah, and Amy Slipowitz, *Freedom in the World, 2022: The Global Expansion of Authoritarian Rule*, Freedom House, 2022.

Riccucci, Norma M., and Gregg G. Van Ryzin, "Representative Bureaucracy: A Lever to Enhance Social Equity, Coproduction, and Democracy," *Public Administration Review*, Vol. 77, No. 1, 2017, pp. 21–30.

Rich, Michael D., and Jennifer Kavanagh, "How Biden Can Stop 'Truth Decay' and Restore the Public's Faith in Facts," *Las Vegas Sun*, November 23, 2020.

Rideout, Victoria, Alanna Peebles, Supreet Mann, and Michael B. Robb, *The Common Sense Census: Media Use by Tweens and Teens, 2021*, San Francisco, Calif.: Common Sense, 2022.

Rideout, Victoria J., and Michael B. Robb, *Remote Learning and Digital Equity During the Pandemic*, San Francisco, Calif.: Common Sense Media, 2021.

Rose-Ackerman, Susan, *Corruption and Government: Causes, Consequences, and Reform*, Cambridge University Press, 2012.

Rosenblatt, Alan J., "On-Line Polling: Methodological Limitations and Implications for Electronic Democracy," *Harvard International Journal of Press/Politics*, Vol. 4, No. 2, 1999, pp. 30–44.

Rydgren, Jens, "Social Isolation? Social Capital and Radical Right-Wing Voting in Western Europe," *Journal of Civil Society*, Vol. 5, No. 2, 2009, pp. 129–150.

Salazar, Martha, "State Recognition of American Indian Tribes," National Conference of State Legislatures, October 2016. As of June 2, 2022: https://www.ncsl.org/legislators-staff/legislators/quad-caucus/ state-recognition-of-american-indian-tribes.aspx

Schaeffer, Katherine, "Racial, Ethnic Diversity Increases Yet Again with the 117th Congress," Pew Research Center, January 28, 2021a. As of June 1, 2022: https://www.pewresearch.org/fact-tank/2021/01/28/ racial-ethnic-diversity-increases-yet-again-with-the-117th-congress/

———, "The Changing Face of Congress in 7 Charts," Pew Research Center, March 10, 2021b. As of June 1, 2022: https://www.pewresearch.org/fact-tank/2021/03/10/ the-changing-face-of-congress/

Schlachter, Laura Hanson, *Key Findings from the 2019 Current Population Survey: Civic Engagement and Volunteering Supplement*, Washington, D.C.: AmeriCorps, Office of Research and Evaluation, 2021.

Schugurensky, Daniel, and John P. Myers, "Informal Civic Learning Through Engagement in Local Democracy: The Case of the Seniors' Task Force of Healthy City Toronto," in Kathryn Church, Nina Bascia, and Eric Shragge, eds., *Learning Through Community: Exploring Participatory Practices*, Springer, 2008, pp. 73–95.

Schwartz, Sarah, "Map: Where Critical Race Theory Is Under Attack," *EdWeek*, September 2022.

Shah, Dhavan V., Nojin Kwak, and Robert Lance Holbert, "'Connecting' and 'Disconnecting' with Civic Life: Patterns of Internet Use and the Production of Social Capital," *Political Communication*, Vol. 18, No. 2, 2001, pp. 141–162.

Shapiro, Sarah, and Catherine Brown, "The State of Civics Education," Center for American Progress, February 21, 2018. As of June 1, 2022: https://www.americanprogress.org/article/state-civics-education/

Sirianni, Carmen, and Lewis Friedland, *Civic Innovation in America: Community Empowerment, Public Policy, and the Movement for Civic Renewal*, University of California Press, 2001.

Skinnell, Ryan, "A Good Democracy Requires Disagreement, Conflict, and Argument," *The Fulcrum*, October 7, 2020.

Stern, Jeremy A., Alison E. Brody, Jose A. Gregory, Stephen Griffith, and Jonathan Pulvers, *The State of State Standards for Civics and U.S. History in 2021*, Thomas B. Fordham Institute, 2021.

Stout, Cathryn, and Thomas Wilburn, "CRT Map: Efforts to Restrict Teaching Racism and Bias Have Multiplied Across the U.S.," *Chalkbeat*, February 1, 2022. As of June 1, 2022: https://www.chalkbeat.org/22525983/ map-critical-race-theory-legislation-teaching-racism

Sullivan, Margaret, "What Happens to Democracy When Local Journalism Dries Up?" *Washington Post*, November 30, 2021.

Tableau Public, "Do You Live in a News Desert?" data tool, June 1, 2020. As of June 2, 2022: https://public.tableau.com/app/profile/unccislm1164/viz/ NewspapersByCountyUnitedStates/DesertandOne

Tate, Katherine, *Black Faces in the Mirror: African Americans and Their Representatives in the U.S. Congress*, Princeton University Press, 2004.

Theobald, Nick A., and Donald P. Haider-Markel, "Race, Bureaucracy, and Symbolic Representation: Interactions Between Citizens and Police," *Journal of Public Administration Research and Theory*, Vol. 19, 2008, pp. 409–426.

Thorson, Kjerstin, Yu Xu, and Stephanie Edgerly, "Political Inequalities Start at Home: Parents, Children, and the Socialization of Civic Infrastructure Online," *Political Communication*, Vol. 35, No. 2, 2018, pp. 178–195.

Tolbert, Caroline J., and Ramona S. McNeal, "Unraveling the Effects of the Internet on Political Participation?" *Political Research Quarterly*, Vol. 56, No. 2, 2003, pp. 175–185.

Torney-Purta, Judith, Julio C. Cabrera, Katrina Crotts Roohr, Ou Lydia Liu, and Joseph A. Rios, *Assessing Civic Competency and Engagement in Higher Education: Research Background, Frameworks, and Directions for Next-Generation Assessment*, ETS Research Report Series, Vol. 2015, No. 2, 2015, pp. 1–48.

Townsend, Rebecca M., "Town Meeting as a Communication Event: Democracy's Act Sequence," *Research on Language and Social Interaction*, Vol. 42, No. 1, 2009, pp. 68–89.

Transparency International, Corruption Perceptions Index, data tool, undated. As of June 12, 2022:
https://www.transparency.org/en/cpi/2020

———, "2020 Corruption Perceptions Index Reveals Widespread Corruption Is Weakening COVID-19 Response, Threatening Global Recovery," January 28, 2021. As of June 1, 2022:
https://www.transparency.org/en/press/
2020-corruption-perceptions-index-reveals-widespread-corruption-is-
weakening-covid-19-response-threatening-global-recovery

Trust for Public Land, "How Does Your City's ParkScore Rating Stack Up?" data tool, undated. As of June 1, 2022:
https://www.tpl.org/parkscore

Tynes, Brendesha M., Elizabeth Leal García, Michael T. Giang, and Nicola Coleman, "The Racial Landscape of Social Networking Sites: Forging Identity, Community, and Civic Engagement," *I/S: A Journal of Law and Policy for the Information Society*, Vol. 7, No. 1, 2011.

United Nations, "Democracy," webpage, undated. As of June 1, 2022:
https://www.un.org/en/global-issues/democracy

———, Universal Declaration of Human Rights, December 8, 1948.

United States Election Project, homepage, undated. As of June 2, 2022:
https://www.electproject.org/

University of North Carolina Hussman School of Journalism and Media, "Do You Live in a News Desert?" webpage, undated. As of June 2, 2022:
https://www.usnewsdeserts.com/

U.S. Census Bureau, "Explore Census Data," data tool, undated. As of June 2, 2022:
https://data.census.gov/cedsci/

———, *Current Population Survey, September 2019: Volunteering and Civic Life Supplement, Technical Documentation CPS—19*, Washington, D.C., 2019.

———, "Voting and Registration in the Election of November 2020," webpage, April 2021a. As of June 10, 2022:
https://www.census.gov/data/tables/time-series/demo/voting-and-registration/p20-585.html

———, "Historical Reported Voting Rates," data tool, October 6, 2021b. As of June 2, 2022:
https://www.census.gov/data/tables/time-series/demo/voting-and-registration/voting-historical-time-series.html

Valenzuela, Sebastián, Yonghwan Kim, and Homero Gil de Zúñiga, "Social Networks That Matter: Exploring the Role of Political Discussion for Online Political Participation," *International Journal of Public Opinion Research,* Vol. 24, No. 2, 2011, pp. 163–184.

van Deth, Jan W., "Studying Political Participation: Towards a Theory of Everything?" paper presented at Joint Sessions of Workshops of the European Consortium for Political Research, Grenoble, France, 2001.

van Deth, Jan W., and Sonja Zmerli, "Introduction: Civicness, Equality, and Democracy—A 'Dark Side' of Social Capital?" *American Behavioral Scientist,* Vol. 53, No. 5, 2010, pp. 631–639.

van Holm, Eric Joseph, "Unequal Cities, Unequal Participation: The Effect of Income Inequality on Civic Engagement," *American Review of Public Administration,* Vol. 49, No. 2, 2019, pp. 135–144.

Vinnakota, Raj, *From Civic Education to a Civic Learning Ecosystem: A Landscape Analysis and Case for Collaboration,* Red & Blue Works, 2019.

Williams, Jhacova A., Trevon D. Logan, and Bradley L. Hardy, "The Persistence of Historical Racial Violence and Political Suppression: Implications for Contemporary Regional Inequality," *The ANNALS of the American Academy of Political and Social Science,* Vol. 694, No. 1, 2021, pp. 92–107.

Wojcieszak, Magdalena E., and Diana C. Mutz, "Online Groups and Political Discourse: Do Online Discussion Spaces Facilitate Exposure to Political Disagreement?," *Journal of Communication,* Vol. 59, No. 1, 2009, pp. 40–56.

Wolfe, David Allan, "Civic Governance, Social Learning and the Strategic Management of City-Regions," in David B. Audretsch and Mary L. Walshok, eds., *Creating Competitiveness: Entrepreneurship and Innovation Policies for Growth,* Edward Elgar, 2012.

Wood, Wendy, Jessica Baen, and Ken Cloke, "Foundations for Building Conflict Literacy," webpage, Democracy, Politics, and Conflict Engagement, 2019. As of June 1, 2022:
https://www.dpaceinitiative.org/conflict-literacy-framework/foundations/

Ye, Yinjiao, Ping Xu, and Mingxin Zhang, "Social Media, Public Discourse and Civic Engagement in Modern China," *Telematics Informatics,* Vol. 34, 2017, pp. 705–714.

Zimmerman, Joseph Francis, *The New England Town Meeting: Democracy in Action,* Greenwood Publishing Group, 1999.